DUMB MONEY

*How Our Greatest Financial Minds
Bankrupted the Nation*

Daniel Gross

Free Press

NEW YORK LONDON TORONTO SYDNEY

Free Press

A Division of Simon & Schuster, Inc.

1230 Avenue of the Americas

New York, NY 10020

This Free Press paperback edition April 2009

FREE PRESS and colophon are trademarks of Simon & Schuster, Inc.

For information about special discounts for bulk purchases,
please contact Simon & Schuster Special Sales at 1-866-506-1949
or business@simonandschuster.com.

The Simon & Schuster Speakers Bureau can bring authors to
your live event. For more information or to book an event contact
the Simon & Schuster Speakers Bureau at 1-866-248-3049
or visit our website at www.simonspeakers.com.

Designed by Paul Dippolito

Manufactured in the United States of America

3 5 7 9 10 8 6 4 2

Library of Congress Cataloging-in-Publication Data is available.

ISBN-13: 978-1-4391-5987-3
ISBN-10:   1-4391-5987-4

Contents

DUMB MONEY

CHAPTER I

WTF?

Last November, high-rolling developer Donald Trump's company was scheduled to pay the $334 million balance on a $640 million loan from a group of lenders led by Deutsche Bank, which had been extended to build a glitzy 92-story condominium tower in Chicago, named (what else?) Trump Tower. But sales had been slow because the city's high-end condo market was suffering from the economic downturn. Seeking an extension of the loan, Trump sued the lenders, invoking *force majeure*, a standard clause in loan documents that permits developers to put off completing projects if an unexpected cataclysm takes place—a flood, a strike, a riot, a mammoth sinkhole, a meteor, or "any other event or circumstance not within the reasonable control of the borrower." In Trump's view, the economy had suffered just such an event. "A depression is not within the control of the borrower," as the author of *Think Big and Kick Ass in Business and Life* put it.

Later the same month, former secretary of the Treasury Robert Rubin, the yin to Trump's yang—understated, publicity-ducking, with a hair shade in the normal color spectrum—was trying to salvage his declining reputation. In the 1990s, as a member of what became known as the Committee to Save the World, Rubin had helped avert a series of financial crises. The former Goldman Sachs arbitrager had spent most of this decade as a highly paid vice chairman and key adviser at Citigroup, the giant bank that has become a charter member of the Committee to Bankrupt the World. Citigroup had racked up tens of billions of dollars in losses on subprime bonds, mortgages, new instruments called collateralized debt obligations, leveraged loans, credit card loans—oh, to hell with it, pretty much every kind of debt. "In hindsight, there are a lot of things we'd do differently," Rubin said as part of a press offensive. "But in the context of the facts as I knew them and my role, I'm inclined to think probably not." After all, he told *Newsweek*, Citi and the financial system had suffered "the perfect storm." Rubin left Citigroup in January.

More than anybody, Alan Greenspan was the intellectual architect of this decade's economy. A good-luck mascot of two bull markets, the longtime Federal Reserve chairman had spent his career evangelizing for the Holy Trinity: low interest rates, deregulated markets, and the ability of financial innovation to insulate markets and the millions of people who depended on them from calamities. However, when he appeared before Congress in October, Greenspan expressed doubts about his theories on the magic of markets. "I found a flaw," he said. "I was shocked because I had been going for forty years or more with very considerable evidence that it was working exceptionally well." A flaw? The persistence of low interest rates—that, Greenspan assured us, made all the sense in the world—sparked a speculative orgy in securities and derivatives. These instruments, he had assured us, would help people manage risk; instead, they created systemic risk. Deregulated, free, and open markets had gone so haywire that they required massive government intervention. *Pretty much everything Greenspan said about how this system was supposed to work was wrong!* In fact, it is now clear that because of the way the system was designed, losses and failures could only create massive, widely distributed losses. The disaster was not a bug, but an inevitable feature of the financial operating code Greenspan had helped write.

Within a few months in the summer and fall of 2008, financial players large and small, rogues and respected elders, blue collar and white shoe, suffered a host of stunning, appalling, nauseating *forces majeures*, a deluge of Category 5 perfect storms. When the subprime lending industry began to go tapioca in early

2007, the authorities assured us that the financial problems were confined to the unsavory business of making high-interest loans to marginal individual borrowers. But a year later, as the presidential election careened toward its frenzied finish, the lethal virus had infected the nation's entire financial system. The government nationalized the two largest lending institutions, Fannie Mae (the Federal National Mortgage Association) and Freddie Mac (the Federal Home Loan Mortgage Corporation), and effectively took control of the nation's largest insurance company, AIG (American International Group), by extending more than $100 billion in loans to the stricken company. The nation's fourth-largest investment bank, Lehman Brothers, filed for Chapter 11, triggering a gut-wrenching chain of events that forced the federal government to step in and guarantee money-market mutual funds, heretofore the safest place to stow cash this side of a mattress. Giant commercial banks, including Washington Mutual and Wachovia, effectively failed, with the Federal Deposit Insurance Corporation (FDIC) brokering their sales, at nominal prices, to larger banks. A couple dozen smaller banks simply were eaten by the FDIC, whose primary role is to insure deposits in banks and thrift institutions. In September, after a few tense weeks of negotiations and grinding market volatility, Congress approved a $700 billion bailout of the nation's financial system. But Treasury Secretary Henry M. Paulson's plan to deploy that cash to buy toxic mortgages was quickly abandoned in favor of injecting funds directly into large banks. Not to be outdone, the Federal Reserve committed $500 billion to buy mortgage-backed securities issued by Fannie Mae and Freddie Mac, and also offered to backstop commercial paper and other debt issuance by private companies. Because foreign investors traded heavily in mortgage-backed securities, the financial agony went global. In the last quarter of 2008, staid British banks, grasping Russian oligarchs, German corporate monarchs, French finance companies, and Spanish home lenders began to falter from the most deadly infection to hit the Continent since the bubonic plague of 1348. Iceland's banking system, which had amassed foreign currency debt equal to eight times its gross domestic product, keeled over, plunging the entire island nation into bankruptcy. The potential cost (so far) to America's taxpayers? Up to $8 trillion and counting.

Meanwhile, back in the real world—the shrinking portion of the economy not controlled by the government—large companies like Linens'n Things and the Tribune Company, staggering under debt loads piled onto them by private equity buyers, went bankrupt. Hedge funds, the exclusive investment vehicles for the ultrarich that had come to dominate the money culture, began to block investors from withdrawing cash, lest the funds be forced into liquidation. A decade of rising inequality is being capped off by an oddly egalitarian moment wherein the private equity firm that owns Chrysler and the automaker's workers are suffering proportional losses. The cherry on top of this miserable sundae: in December, former NASDAQ chairman Bernard Madoff, whose investment firm had quietly racked up steady (too steady, it turns out) returns for well-heeled clients for decades, revealed that his $50 billion empire was nothing more than a Ponzi scheme. From Trump on down, it seems, everybody who thought big this century has gotten his ass kicked.

Humble observers cannot indulge in too much *Trumpenfreude* (joy at Donald Trump's suffering) because the damage has spread to the real economy. The financial system's failures have frozen credit, leading to plunging auto and retail sales, rising corporate bankruptcies, an upsurge in unemployment, massive deficits, and a level of unfocused economic dread not seen since the 1930s. All of which left a big stinking mess for the incoming president. "Black Man Given Nation's Worst Job," *The Onion* blared on November 5, 2008.

WTF? How did the Ownership Society devolve so quickly into Bailout Nation? What turned the Bush Boom—a period of low interest rates, rising asset prices, and economic growth—into Hoover 2.0? How did the crown jewel of American capitalism—our financial services industry—transform into cubic zirconium? What happened?

This brief book—a long essay that is more a chronicle of this decade's money culture than an investigation into the fetid nooks and crannies of the financial system—attempts to answer these questions. The answer is at once relatively simple and somewhat complicated.

First things first. There are elements of the truth to the *mea exculpas* of Trump, Rubin, and Greenspan. The disasters were the results of massive natural forces, and they did constitute a perfect storm. There is plenty of blame to go around: poor regulation, eight years of a failed Republican economic philosophy, Wall Street–friendly Democrats who helped stymie reform, misguided bipartisan efforts to promote home ownership, Wall Street greed, corrupt CEOs, a botched rescue effort. Uncle Alan Greenspan certainly played a big role. And so did his successor, Ben Bernanke. However, to argue that any one person is responsible for the mess is fatuous. That does not mean we should remove human agency from the equation. Far from it. The debacle was the byproduct of conscious acts of millions of men and women pursuing their self-interests. If Countrywide Financial CEO Angelo Mozilo had not spearheaded a culture of reckless mortgage lending, somebody else would have. Unsophisticated borrowers who took loans they couldn't afford to pay back bear some responsibility, although the sophisticated finance professionals who made that culture of lending possible deserve much more of the blame. This is the *High School Musical* of financial debacles: we're all in this together. All of us—investors, home owners, borrowers, lenders, journalists, elected officials, economists, regulators, credit rating agencies—helped assemble this multi-trillion-dollar "crap sandwich," as House minority leader John Boehner memorably dubbed the situation.

A second point. The manifold investigations now underway surely will turn up plenty of criminal behavior. But the scandal of the decade will not be the losses created by swindlers and con artists. No, the real scandal is that law-abiding, respectable citizens who were operating well within the confines of laws and regulations racked up the overwhelming majority of losses suffered. A $1.2 trillion subprime mortgage market? A $62 trillion unregulated, nontransparent credit default swap market? Publicly held investment banks holding huge quantities of CDOs, CMBS, RMBS, CLOs, and other securities that their CEOs, CFOs, and CIOs could neither understand nor value? Turning subprime bonds into AAA-rated bonds through a form of credit alchemy? Negative amortization loans made to people without documentation? Fifty-billion-dollar private equity buyouts of cyclical companies? Hedge funds going public? Well, it all seemed like a good idea at the time. In fact, the players building these new businesses were lionized as geniuses, as transformational business figures, as experts on retailing, philanthropy, and politics. They were the Smart Money.

So here's how I would frame the past eight years. An Era of Cheap Money devolved into an Era of Dumb Money, and then down to an Era of Dumber Money. In the midst of a debt-fueled orgy, the ethics, business model, and mentality of Dumb Money infused our culture, politics, and economic life. Because economic reality always catches up with economic stupidity, the vast easy-money sector—industries that thrive on access to cheap and plentiful credit, like insurance, housing, banking, investment banking, and auto manufacturing—has just exploded.

Of course, vast impersonal global forces did play a big role in this drama. Inside the petri dish of unique macroeconomic economic circumstances, a powerful bubble-blowing agent interacted with a potent catalyst in a chain reaction that produced significant benefits before blowing up spectacularly.

The rapidly changing economic geography of the world ush-

ered in an era of imbalances. The relocation of American manufacturing to China, coupled with rising oil prices, meant that the
United States shipped hundreds of billions of dollars abroad each
year. These dollars returned to our shores in the form of foreign
purchases of safe assets—for example, bonds issued by the government and government-sponsored enterprises. The result was
what Alan Greenspan called "the conundrum": the persistence
of low long-term interest rates amid inflationary pressures. And
as US central bankers came to fear deflation more than they did
inflation, they slashed short-term rates aggressively and kept
them low. In the years after 9/11, these two big-picture trends
created plentiful credit at historically low rates—an Era of Cheap
Money that lasted from late 2001 through 2004.

Benign at the outset, the Era of Cheap Money sparked an in-
ferno of housing and credit speculation that raged from 2004
through 2007. The kindling was there all along: America's pro-
pensity to embrace new economic trends and create bubbles.
This decade saw a replay of the dynamic seen in the 1990s with
speculation in dotcom start-ups, and with the emergnce of the
telegraph in 1840s. I have argued elsewhere (in my 2007 book
Pop! Why Bubbles Are Great for the Economy) that this process
produces beneficial results when it leaves behind a new commercial infrastructure. Without the debacles of telecommunica-
tions companies WorldCom and Global Crossing, there would
have been no Google. (Alas, 26,000-square-foot spec mansions in
Greenwich do not count as new commercial infrastructure.) During bubbles, investors latch on to new economic assumptions
(see above) and new technologies (in this case securitization, derivatives, and funky mortgages). The government chips in with
an assist through policies and incentives that channel investment
into the hot new areas (for example, the home-mortgage deduction, and preferential tax treatment for capital gains and hedge
fund income). Investors project recent growth endlessly into the
future, in an attempt to justify investment at any level, and the

culture banishes bad news and elevates shills to prophets. The three "i"s appear on the scene: the innovators, the imitators, and finally the idiots.

But here is what is commonly misunderstood: the bubble was not just in housing. It was in debt, in speculation, in gambling. "At the center of this crisis was a bubble of risk taking," said money manager Jeremy Grantham. Ultimately, this bubble was produced by two related phenomena: the culture of Wall Street and the rise of what became known as the Shadow Banking system, whose unregulated financial institutions included investment banks and hedge funds. Together they induced a spree of reckless, largely unregulated lending, borrowing, and trading, one that preferred short-term fees to long-term gains, that valued racking up capital gains over preserving reputations, and that confused liquidity with access to other people's money. For the sake of convenience, I've coined the term "Hedge Fund Nation" to describe the process and activities through which the values and ethos of Wall Street's new major players upended traditional business models and permeated the financial sector and the culture at large.

Wall Street has always been instrumental to the formation of bubbles. In the 1990s, Silicon Valley hit upon the commercial potential of the internet, but it took Wall Street to turn it into initially brilliant but ultimately disastrous investments. The same held here. Mortgages became the raw material for new types of investment products (mortgage-backed securities and packages of mortgage-backed securities called collateralized debt obligations) that could be chopped up, sold to investors who paid for them with borrowed money, and then traded, again with borrowed money. Enthralled with the lure of cheap money, storied investment banks that for generations had been content to service clients, suddenly turned into hedge funds, borrowing huge sums of money to make investments for their own accounts.

Every component of the regulatory apparatus in Washington—the White House, the Treasury Department, the Federal Reserve, the Securities and Exchange Commission, Congress—failed to diagnose the bad debt virus. In some quarters, there is a sense that the whole mess should be laid at the feet of Fannie Mae and Freddie Mac, the failed mortgage giants that owned or guaranteed about half the nation's housing debt, and the Community Reinvestment Act (CRA), a law passed during the Carter administration that required banks to lend to the poor communities in which they took deposits. However, the most salient fact about this debacle is that the regulated commercial banks were frequently bit players. The biggest subprime lenders that failed—outfits such as Argent Mortgage and American Home Mortgage—were not regulated by the Federal Reserve. These institutions worked hand in glove with Bear Stearns and Lehman Brothers, entities to which the CRA and other federal banking regulations likewise did not apply. Before it collapsed, Bear Stearns had $33 in debt for every dollar of capital—ensuring that a 3 percent decline in its assets would wipe out the firm. The CRA did not force mortgage companies to offer loans for no money down, or force the credit-rating agencies to slap high-grade ratings on packages of subprime debt, or force hedge funds to trade those securities. AIG did not plunge into the credit-default-swaps business with abandon because Association of Community Organizations for Reform Now (ACORN) members picketed its offices. And no government forced a hedge fund and banks to lend hundreds of millions of dollars to Donald Trump. The huge, aggressive Shadow Banking system—composed of Wall Street investment banks, private equity firms, hedge funds, unregulated lending businesses of all sizes, insurance companies, and individuals—inflated the risk-taking bubble. The dumb-lending virus originated in midtown Manhattan, Greenwich, Connecticut, and Southern California, not Brownsville, Washington, DC, and East Los Angeles.

How could it be that, save for a few hedge fund managers, virtually none of the obscenely paid, highly experienced, intelligent Wall Street big shots like Robert Rubin took evasive action? Even Goldman Sachs, the elite among Wall Street elite, has taken its lumps. "As long as the music is playing, you've got to get up and dance," is the way former Citigroup CEO Chuck Prince put it in the summer of 2007, explaining why his firm was still committing to huge loans when things were plainly out of control. That neatly encapsulates the problematic culture of Wall Street. As long as fees are available and money is to be made, nobody blows the whistle. People who stand up amid a bubble and yell stop will be made to look foolish if the bubble lasts for just one quarter. Every crappy dotcom initial public offering (IPO) that Merrill Lynch passed over in 1999 was one that Goldman Sachs picked up. Besides, it worked brilliantly. Massive leverage allowed investment banks to turn decent trading ideas into home runs. It allowed private equity funds to take control of a company, have it issue $500 million in bonds, and use the cash to pay the new owners a $500 million dividend. Easy and dumb money is reinforcing. For more than two and a half years, between June 2004 and February 2007, not a single bank failed, and this gave financial institutions the courage to commit greater sums to transactions of all types. As default rates on corporate debt plummeted, the Smart Money crowd—Citigroup, Merrill Lynch—committed to the equivalent of no-money-down corporate loans, extending hundreds of billions of dollars in credit to private equity firms for leveraged buyouts, and then picked up fees both for making the loans and for selling them off. If one bank would not do it, another one would. And if no bank would do it, a hedge fund or a private equity firm would.

The post–Dumb Money era has been humbling, not just for Donald Trump, Robert Rubin, and Alan Greenspan. Though the innovators cashed out early, many of the imitators have been exposed as idiots. Floating in the bubble, players were elevated to rock stars, geniuses, and celebrities simply because of their ability to use leverage. Now stripped of their easy access to financing, they seem quite common. Henry Paulson, lionized by some (okay, by this writer) as King Henry, the *über*-competent former Goldman Sachs CEO running the financial system, quickly shifted to a clueless groper in the dark. "When you grow up, you think the people in charge actually know the answers," said David Rothkopf, author of *Superclass: The Global Power Elite and the World They Are Making*, when asked about the seemingly stunning reversal in Paulson's reputation. "The real unsettling big truth is that they're the same people you went to high school with." Of course, nothing about Paulson—or Trump, or Rubin, or Greenspan, or any of us—fundamentally changed in 2008. Rather, in the grips of a set of delusions, all of us made some basic, disastrous miscalculations. Alan Greenspan has noticed that this storm we have just lived through is a "once-in-a-century credit tsunami." Paulson has said that this sort of thing happens "once or twice" every hundred years. What is the difference between once and twice? In this instance, several trillion dollars in losses.

All we can do now, aside from rage at our vanished home equity, shrinking portfolios, and booming national debt, is try to understand what happened, and why, and how we might avoid a repeat.

Let's begin.

CHAPTER II

The Era of Cheap Money

The economic and financial story of this decade began not on January 1, 2000, but on two dates in 2001. At some point in March 2001, the economy began to contract, entering a brief recession and bringing to an end the longest expansion in American history. About six months later, the events of 9/11 definitively pierced the bubbles of American supremacy and shiny, happy globalization. Somewhere in between, we reached an important inflection point and shifted from the Ownership Society to the Debtorship Society, from an era of Reasonably Priced Money to an era of Cheap Money. During the three years after 9/11, the intellectual foundations and industrial scaffolding of the Dumb Money edifice were laid.

Bubbles require two essential and mutually reinforcing ingredients: a new set of economic assumptions and a new set of exciting technologies. In the 1990s, the turbines of growth were the promise of low inflation, a highly productive globalized economy, and the communications technologies that made the New Economy possible. This decade, the driving forces were a set of economic assumptions—some new, some extrapolations from 1990s trends—and a relatively new set of technologies that promised to spread, distribute, manage, and ultimately banish risk from financial transactions. Together, these strands of code, intertwined like a double helix, created a new economic operating system that made virtues of our vices and made cheap money seem eminently sensible.

In homage to Thomas Friedman, let's dub this decade's economic component Flat World Economics. (In further homage to

Friedman, let's abbreviate that to FWE.) Flat World Economists provided an intellectual framework for understanding why money, which was already cheap, should stay cheap and get even cheaper, and why it was acceptable—even desirable—for the United States to start guzzling debt the way fraternity boys pound beers on spring break.

Despite the dotcom bust, the United States economy survived the 1990s in rather good shape. Strong broad-based growth had thrown off lots of taxes, so the government was running a budget surplus. The national debt was starting to shrink. An Ownership Society had evolved from rhetoric to reality. By 2000, 52 percent of American households owned stock, up from about 25 percent in 1990, spurred by the 401(k) revolution, the rise of online brokers, and a bull market. About 67 percent of Americans owned their homes, and they had a big chunk of equity in them; the nation's housing stock was saddled in 2001 with $5.6 trillion in mortgage debt. At the end of 2000, the nation's total household debt was $7.01 trillion, or 71.4 percent of GDP (gross domestic product). Americans saved 5.82 cents on every dollar they earned. And money was cheap by historical standards. The federal funds rate—the short-term interest rate that the central bank controls—stood at 6.5 percent at the end of 2000, and the 30-year bond, one of the benchmarks from which long-term mortgage rates were set, paid 5.5 percent interest. These rates were sharply lower than the prevailing rates of the late 1980s and early 1990s. The mortgage market's muscle memory had kept rates elevated long after Paul Volcker, the cigar-chomping Federal Reserve chairman, launched a jihad on inflation by jacking up interest rates into the high double digits in the late 1970s. (My bar mitzvah money in 1980 went into a money market fund that paid an outrageous 18 percent.)

In the 1990s, with maestro Alan Greenspan conducting monetary policy, the fed funds rate ranged between 3 percent and 6 percent, though the bias always seemed toward lower rates, for two reasons. First, the hyperrationalist, data-driven central banker in the mid-1990s took an uncharacteristic leap of faith into the New Economy, testing the hypothesis that heightened productivity, globalization, and information technology would allow for higher growth without inflation. Second, Greenspan's preferred response to virtually every crisis—from the Asian meltdown of 1997 to the 9/11 attacks—was to lower the price of money. Investors' belief that Greenspan would always do so helped put a floor under stocks. "Do you mean, was there a Greenspan put?" he asked rhetorically when, in October 2007, I interviewed him in his DuPont Circle office. He was a small, shuffling, extremely soft-spoken figure who possessed none of the imperium that had accompanied his appearances before Congress. (The answer conveyed by his enigmatic smile was a qualified "yes.") The expectation that short-term interest rates would stay low and could always go lower, especially in times of stress, became part of investors' calculus. The principal architect of the Era of Cheap Money aggressively cut rates in 2001 as the economy slowed. But between 9/11 and June 2003, as Greenspan attempted to jolt the traumatized economy back into life, he played interest rate limbo, hacking the fed funds rate from 3 percent in September 2001 to 1 percent in June 2003, and then leaving it there for a year. Considered another way, the price of short-term money for banks fell by 85 percent in thirty months.

Influential and instrumental as he was, Greenspan controlled only short-term rates. Long-term interest rates, the types that determined what people would pay for mortgages, were set by the market. And between 2002 and 2004, *mirabile dictu*, they seemed to follow suit even in the face of solid global growth, inflationary pressures, and sharp increases in US government and trade deficits—trends that usually push rates up. Greenspan labeled this conundrum "the conundrum." In a June 2005 speech delivered via satellite to a conference in China (a perfect example of new technology and globalization-enhancing productivity),

Greenspan described the "remarkable worldwide environment of low long-term interest rates."

During bubbles, we always develop a series of intellectual justifications to "explain" why the rules have changed, or why the old rules no longer apply. Remember the contortions internet analysts went through to place reasonable values on companies possessing no earnings and scant revenues? It was no different in the Era of Cheap Money. The first tenet of FWE—the Circularity of Money—helped explain the conundrum.

America's negative balance of payments—the difference between the amount of goods and services we import and those we export—began to spike in this decade. The manufacturing base continued to go offshore, especially to China. And as domestic energy production declined from 53 percent of daily consumption in 1995 to 42 percent in 2004, oil imports soared. Every day, Americans shipped billions of dollars abroad to buy plastic and metal stuff from Shenzhen province and gooey liquid stuff from the Ghawar oil fields. The trade deficit (balance of payments) rose from $108 billion in 1997 to $365 billion in 2001, and would nearly double to $711 billion in 2005. Between 1998 and 2006, imports more than doubled while exports rose only 56 percent. Such imbalances are not necessarily problematic because money is circular. And all those dollars we shipped abroad had to return to America's shores through various transactions—a Japanese tourist splurging at Disney World or a German company buying Oracle software. But the most significant deals were executed by the Chinese central bank and Persian Gulf investment funds.

Politics, customs, and culture led these two major recipients of dollars—who were generally nondemocratic, nontransparent, non-Western, and risk averse—to buy government bonds, not stocks or companies or other hard American assets. (When a Dubai-based company tried to buy a company that operated US ports in 2006, Congress went all Jack Bauer and killed the deal.) The Chinese government kept its currency at a fixed, weak exchange rate vis-à-vis the dollar (the better to promote exports) by taking dollars received for goods and buying dollar-denominated assets. Persian Gulf nations, who similarly pegged their currency to the dollar, likewise viewed US government bonds as bullet-proof, noncontroversial investments. So the shape of the global economy and the rising volume of trade created a virtuous circle. The biggest recipients of exported dollars simply had to buy US government bonds, no matter how little they yielded. Their constant purchases helped push prices up and long-term interest rates down even further. From 2000 to 2003, 30-year mortgage rates dropped by nearly a third, from 8.5 percent to 6 percent.

A bond yielding 4 percent becomes worth less if inflation spikes from 2 percent to 4 percent. And so FWE developed a second tenet that would provide assurance to the People's Bank of China and the Persian Gulf oil sultanates. Since the 1970s, US central bankers, their sleep haunted by memories of Carter-era stagflation, the lethal combination of low growth and high inflation, had generally quaked at the prospects of inflation. By this decade, however, central bankers had internalized the message of the Volcker-Greenspan legacy—that inflation had been forever crushed. And when a global slowdown took hold in 2001, a new meme emerged to suggest that we might have as much to fear from deflation as from inflation.

The leading explicator of the shifting mind-set was Ben Bernanke, a Princeton economist who became a member of the Federal Reserve's Board of Governors in August 2002. Bernanke specialized in the Great Depression, a time when falling asset prices destroyed the financial system, so he knew from deflation. In a November 2002 speech to the National Economists Club on the topic, Bernanke took pains to say he did not think deflation was an impending risk. Why? If the system were to catch a whiff of the dread disease, the central bank would emulate Malcolm X. "I am confident that the Fed would take whatever means necessary to prevent significant deflation in the United States," he said, citing economist Milton Friedman's line that, in case of de-flation, the central bank should stand ready to drop money from helicopters. Two key points arose from this. First, if we were in an environment where deflation was even a potential risk, then lower-than-expected interest rates made all the sense in the world. Second, should deflation materialize, the world's leading central bank would be expected to provide more cheap money.

Bernanke was also a leading intellectual exponent of the third tenet of FWE. Conventional wisdom held that large US budget and trade deficits arose because Americans preferred to spend rather than save—the savings rate (net savings as a percentage of gross national income) would fall to 1.1 percent in 2003. But chastising Americans for profligacy made sense only if you viewed the United States as an economic island. What if the world were a single, integrated economy? And what if, as in this country, some areas pinched so many pennies that other citizens had to spend like drunken sailors to keep the nation's shops and factories humming? In that case, our great vice—overconsump-tion—would be something of a selfless act of charity. That is precisely the case Bernanke would make in an April 2005 speech, arguing that America's twin deficits could be traced not to a dearth of savings but to a glut of foreign savings. In the rich in-dustrialized countries with graying populations and slow growth (think Old Europe and Japan), people needed to save more for retirement but couldn't find attractive domestic investment op-portunities in their lame, stagnant economies. Japan, in particu-lar, was the Saudi Arabia of savings. Meanwhile, China and other rapidly growing countries in Asia and Latin America that lacked Western safety nets responded to the financial crises of the 1990s by putting controls on capital flows, building up reserves of for-eign currency, and encouraging their citizens to save more. As the volume of trade rose, newly industrializing countries like China, Bernanke said, had metamorphosed "from a net user to a net supplier of funds to international capital markets." Add a rise in oil and other commodity prices, and there was a lot of money sloshing around the developing world just looking for a safe home. Because the United States remained such a comparatively attractive place to invest—even after the NASDAQ meltdown—a lot of that capital was finding its way to America.

Bernanke diplomatically noted that, "in locating the principal causes of the US current account deficit outside the country's borders, I am not making a value judgment about the behavior of either US or foreign residents or their governments." But of course he was. Enough with all the carping about excessive consumption, he seemed to say, tell it to those frugal Chinese. In the face of our fellow global citizens' parsimony, by spending everything we made, and then some, we were simply looking out for the poor Cambodian peasants and the Brazilian farmers. Just as Gap's Red campaign argued, shopping could make you a selfless global citizen. Martin Wolf of the *Financial Times* summed it up best: "In a global economy with no global government, the most important regional power—the US—has been following the Keynesian recommendation by offsetting excess desired savings elsewhere."

And so the US bond market became like a giant carbon offset for otherwise wasteful excess savings. Foreigners' holdings of Treasury securities rose from $1.03 trillion in 2000 to $1.65 trillion in 2004. Net purchases of Treasury bonds by foreign central banks (the difference between the amount bought and sold), rose from $10.7 billion in 2001 to $128.5 billion in 2003. In 2002, non-Americans accounted for about half of net purchases of Treasury securities. But in the first quarter of 2004, they would account for 150 percent! That is—the rest of the world bought a net $679.8 billion in Treasury securities while US brokers and dealers sold a net $202.7 billion. At the end of the first quarter of 2004, according to the Federal Reserve, foreigners owned about 40 percent of outstanding Treasury securities, up from 30 percent in 2000.

As the decade wore on, and US bond yields fell, foreign investors began to seek slightly higher returns. A new class of assets, forged by a new technology, would provide the perfect solution. The rise of securitization was one of the two key technologies—let's call them Network Finance technologies—that spread like wildfire in the Era of Cheap Money. But this innovation was produced by financial engineers, not by software engineers. Securitization is a process through which bankers parcel out risk by chopping up debt—a mortgage, a car loan, a credit card receivable—into pieces that can be bought and sold. (As interest payments on the loan are made, they are passed through to holders of the bonds tied to the mortgages.) Instead of holding on to a loan for 30 years, a bank could make a 30-year mortgage loan, sell it a week later at a small profit, and then put the capital to work again. Securitization turned lending into something like a high-volume manufacturing process.

Government policies always play a role in kicking off bubbles. Congress commissioned the first telegraph line in the 1840s and made huge land grants to railroad builders, setting off an orgy of rail construction. Fannie Mae (founded 1938) and Freddie Mac (founded 1970), the two government-sponsored enterprises that promote home ownership, are often accused of helping to foment the housing bubble by making reckless loans. However, their real contributions to the culture of Dumb Money lie in the way they pioneered the securitization of mortgages.

Fannie and Freddie stood ready to buy mortgages made by banks and other institutions that conformed to certain standards. In the 1970s, the agencies began bundling together mortgages they bought and selling them as bonds. Investors gobbled them up. Why? While the two agencies were nominally private companies (their stock was traded publicly), the market believed that the bonds they issued carried an implied government guarantee. Despite repeated denials by both agencies, investors assumed (correctly, it would turn out) that if things went bad, the federal government would back them up. So the bonds Fannie and Freddie created yielded more than ultrasafe Treasuries but less than corporate bonds, and the securitized mortgages were deemed safe for foreign central banks to buy.

Like Treasury bills, Fannie and Freddie bonds acted like a sponge for the world's excess savings. In 2003, non-US investors held $655 billion of so-called agency or government-sponsored enterprise debt, up from $441 billion in 2000. That was divided among official investors like central banks ($262.9 billion) and private investors ($391.8 billion). With every passing year, the amount of debt held by foreigners—and especially by official foreign investors—rose dramatically. In the first quarter of 2008, foreigners held $1.62 trillion in such debt, or 21 percent of the total. Official authorities hold most of that sum, or $985 billion. Equally important, by creating a robust secondary market for their bonds, Fannie and Freddie set an example for Wall Street. The asset-backed securities market—bonds backed by other types of mortgages that Fannie and Freddie would not buy, like jumbo loans and subprime loans—grew smartly in the Era of Cheap Money. Between 2002 and 2004, the volume of asset-backed securities issuance doubled to $897 billion. And between 2001 and 2006, subprime and Alt-A mortgage issuance quintupled, from about $200 billion to nearly $1 trillion.

A second, related piece of Network Finance technology was at an earlier stage of development: derivatives. Simply defined, a derivative is any security that derives its value from that of another security or asset: a call option on Dell's stock or a futures contract on oil, pork bellies, or presidential candidates. Like nuclear energy, derivatives can be a huge force for good or malevolent ecosystem-destroying monsters. Warren Buffett in 2003 referred to them as "financial weapons of mass destruction." (And no, American soldiers did not find any of those in Iraq either, just cash.) Frank Partnoy, a former derivatives salesman turned law professor and author, argued in his 2003 book *Infec-*

tious Greed that derivatives were responsible for a host of financial calamities in the 1990s, and that their pervasive use rendered "the risk of system-wide collapse . . . greater than ever before." On the other side, Robert Shiller, a Yale economist, saw them as benign volatility-smoothing tools, a new form of insurance against financial risk. In *The New Financial Order: Risk in the 21st Century*, also published in 2003, Shiller envisioned the creation of new social derivative securities: livelihood insurance, through which people could essentially guard against potential income declines, or "macro markets," in which individuals, companies, and central banks could buy and sell securities based on, for example, Peru's 2008 gross domestic product. In time, both Frederich Shiller's "Ode to Joy" and Philip Roth's *Portnoy's Complaint* would be proven prescient.

In every prior bubble, inventors and innovators came up with the hot new idea, and then turned to the nation's money center to monetize it. Modern Wall Street was forged when New York banks raised billions of dollars to finance the late-nineteenth-century railroad boom. In the 1990s, Silicon Valley geeks invented dotcom businesses, but New York investment bankers turned them into crazy investments. In 2001 and 2002, in the aftermath of the dotcom collapse, the Enron scandals, and then New York attorney general Eliot Spitzer's regulatory crusades, the dynamic financial services sector needed a new "new thing." That new thing became debt. The Era of Cheap Money presented Wall Street with a new set of products it could mine, process, package, sell, and trade. Pursuing its own self-interest, Wall Street would use securitization to turn ultracheap money into cheap money for the masses. And the financial sector would start to use derivatives to insure other securities. In the process, Wall Street helped create and stimulate the Cheap Money businesses that would prosper and drive America's impressive post-9/11 recovery.

CHAPTER III

The Cheap Money Economy

Businesses, entrepreneurs, governments, established financial firms, and individuals gave commercial flesh to the dry bones of Cheap Money. It started with the nation's largest manufacturing and retail sector—the auto industry. In the paralyzing week after the 9/11 attacks, Americans remained glued to their televisions and out of the malls. Driven by a mixture of patriotism and desperation—they needed to keep factories humming at high volume and produce revenues to fund their vast liabilities—General Motors extended five-year, interest-free loans for its 2001 and 2002 models. The campaign's slogan "Keep America Rolling" echoed the doomed United Flight 93 passengers' heroic "Let's roll" determination. It also subtly underscored the fact that GM was one of two remaining American car companies. (In a belated act of post–World War II vengeance, Chrysler had been sold to an unsuspecting Daimler in 1998 for $36 billion.) Along with New York mayor Rudy Giuliani, "zero-percent financing" became one of the more enduring and, ultimately, unfortunate post-9/11 symbols. Although its zero-interest loans were originally scheduled to be available for just six weeks, GM would offer some form of free financing for six of the next twelve months. Every time it did, Ford, DaimlerChrysler, and, to a lesser extent, Toyota followed GM's lead. Over the next few years, as customers became conditioned to wait until the Big Three showed them the Cheap Money, this temporary booster shot morphed into a nearly addictive narcotic automakers injected whenever sales lagged.

It worked. Americans bought 16.8 million cars in 2002, and would buy nearly 17 million cars per year for each of the following three years. Car industry sales, which accounted for between 15 percent and 20 percent of US retail sales, had always depended on the availability of credit. Now they became dependent on the availability of essentially free credit. Car dealers and manufacturers convinced themselves that the $17 million annual sales rate was the new normal, despite the extraordinary financing required to maintain it.

Even if they remained buoyant through artificial means, car sales were a rare bright spot. Starting in 2001, business investment, the driving force of the 1990s boom, dried up. As economist Brian Wesbury noted, "Real business fixed investment fell for nine consecutive quarters between the first quarter of 2001 and the first quarter of 2003." Large employers began to implode, especially in the bubbly technology and communications sectors. Enron's failure took down 20,000 jobs, WorldCom's another 60,000. Between March 2001 and June 2003, about 2.66 million payroll jobs were lost, even though the economy started to expand again in November 2001. Economists blamed the sluggish job growth on domestic factors such as high benefit costs and Flat World Economics trends like outsourcing and the rise of the BRIC (Brazil, Russia, India, China) bloc. Large companies such as IBM were cutting back in suddenly slow-growth markets like America as they ramped up activity in suddenly high-growth markets like India. Foreign direct investment outflows jumped from $142 billion in 2001 to $252 billion in 2004. Ordinarily, car sales correlate closely with jobs growth. But—new rule!—car sales rose in a period of sharp job losses because Cheap Money made the cost of buying them go down.

After bubbles, we always look in vain for recovery in the sector that led to the downturn. But technology would take several years to come roaring back. And cars alone could not provide the necessary traction. No, it would have to be something old, something new, something borrowed, and something that would ultimately make a lot of people blue. It would have to be the ultimate Cheap Money business: housing.

For generations, home ownership had been a bedrock of bourgeois financial stability. But four-bedroom Tudors and three-bedroom capes with attached garages were places to live, not cash cows. Over the very long term, between 1890 and 2004, economist Robert Shiller concluded, housing produced a 0.4 percent annual real return. Unlike the internet, this boom would not stem from the introduction of an entirely new technology to the market. In 2001, 67.5 percent of US households owned their abodes. No, the innovation here lay in changing the way people thought about housing. Flat World Economics and the Network Finance industry worked in concert to create a new real estate boom that fit in perfectly with the needs and ethos of the post-9/11, post-dotcom environment.

Housing was the industry most responsive to Cheap Money because of its reliance on debt. Ring the low-interest bell and builders—who buy land, construction materials, and labor with borrowed money—salivate. Purchases are frequently concluded with buyers putting down only 10 percent. America's rising, increasingly mobile population and demographic shifts—to the South and West—created a constant demand for new housing. In the Era of Cheap Money, housing began to boom. Single-family (new home) starts rose smartly, from 1.6 million in 2001 to 2.02 million in 2004, up 26 percent. Existing home sales rose too, from 5.25 million in 2001 to 6.675 million in 2004, up 27 percent. Combined, new and existing home sales in 2004 were 7.86 million, up from 6.15 million in 2001. By the second quarter of 2004, the home ownership rate grew to 69.2 percent, meaning that many millions of people had discovered the joys of property taxes and clogged gutters. After falling from 1989 to 1991, real prices (adjusted for inflation) of homes rose modestly throughout the 1990s, partly due to falling mortgage rates. Yet home values soared in the Era of Cheap Money. The median price for a home rose from $153,000 in 2001 to $195,400 in 2004—up 27.6 percent in three years, a far better return than the stock market.

Given the macroeconomic conditions, this nice little boom could not have happened in a better sector. Virtually all the labor—white collar and blue collar—and most of the materials associated with housing are based in the United States: roofers, the investment bankers who securitize mortgages into bonds, the clerks at Home Depot, mortgage brokers and lawyers, title insurers and deed recorders, appraisers and movers, architects and engineers, interior decorators and plumbers. Northern Trust economist Asha Bangalore concluded in the spring of 2005 that "employment in housing and related industries . . . accounted for about 43 percent of the increase in private sector payrolls since the economic recovery began in November 2001." Between 1998 and 2006, the number of real estate agents rose from 718,000 to 1.37 million, and the number of workers employed by mortgage brokers went from 240,000 in 2000 to 418,700 in 2006.

The expanding legions of mortgage brokers and real estate agents were evangelists for the new housing faith. Thanks to Cheap Money, even as houses were getting more expensive, they were getting cheaper. Paying down an $800,000, 30-year mortgage at 8 percent, the prevailing rate in 2000, cost $5,870 a month. With a 5.6 percent mortgage, the same house cost $4,593 a month—a savings of more than $15,000 per year and $460,000 over 30 years. Just as people who came of financial age in the 1990s believed that stocks moved in only one direction, those who matured financially in the early part of this decade believed that interest rates and housing prices each moved in only one direction (down, and up, respectively). You could overpay for that five-bedroom Toll Brothers McMansion in Totowa, New Jersey, or for that new condo in La Jolla, secure in the knowledge that you could (1) sell it rapidly at a higher price, or (2) change your capital structure, cheaply, at the drop of a hat.

Fueled in large part by technology—mortgage companies became one of the leading advertisers on the web—financing and refinancing became a key part of the money culture. In 1996, the thirty-five brokers at Manhattan Mortgage Company originated about $700 million in mortgages. Pretty good. But in 2003, Manhattan Mortgage's one hundred forty brokers, working out of offices from eastern Long Island to Westchester County, clocked an astonishing $5 billion. Company founder Melissa Cohn, a no-nonsense single mom with large-framed glasses, was the John Henry of mortgage brokers. In 2003, she closed 2,700 loans worth $1.125 billion—more than seven closings per day, every day of the year—earning her the rank of number-two originator of the year from *Mortgage Originator* magazine. "It was insane," Cohn told me in a 2004 interview in which she spoke almost exclusively in short, clipped sentences, one eye continually straying to her email inbox. There was no time for small talk or lengthy discourses when home buyers and refinancers were waiting.

Thanks to falling interest rates and rising home values, home owners found themselves sitting on cash—much as the Beverly Hillbillies discovered black gold in their backyard. The financial service industry's roughnecks were standing by with derricks to help citizens tap into the gushers. Banks and (especially) the rising class of nonbank lenders were happy to lend against the newly discovered reservoirs of home equity. The language and practice of Cheap Money—points, HELOCS, the magic number of basis points it would take to make refinancing work—worked its way into our financial lives, just as surely as AOL and Netscape had in the mid-1990s. The amount of home equity lines of credit (HELOCS) outstanding rose from $420.7 billion in the first quarter of 2000 to $714.8 billion in the first quarter of 2004. Mortgage brokers also urged clients to refinance existing mortgages at lower rates to extract value. Alan Greenspan and Federal Reserve colleague Mark Kennedy began to track the amount of cash that home owners effectively liberated from their bricks and mortar.

In a 2007 paper, they found that mortgage equity withdrawal (MEW), the practice of taking out cash via HELOCs or refinancing, rose from $59.1 billion in the fourth quarter of 2001, or 3.1 percent of disposable income, to $206.7 billion in the third quarter of 2004, or 9.5 percent. In other words, unearned housing-related income became a new source of cash for saving and spending.

But mostly for spending. Even as incomes stagnated, the mighty American consumer was exploring new frontiers. The relentless march of the upscale characterized the Era of Cheap Money. In the fall of 2003, two retail consultants from the Boston Consulting Group published *Trading Up: The New American Luxury*, which nailed the emerging Cheap Money consumer culture. When credit was plentiful and rising home values and falling interest rates did the heavy lifting of earning and saving, everybody felt rich some of the time. The truly rich had no problem paying premium prices for everyday goods, but the rest of us, authors Michael J. Silverstein and Neil Fiske argued, would splurge on items, experiences, or services that tapped into our passions. Hence the aggressive expansion of Starbucks, Williams-Sonoma, Whole Foods, Callaway golf clubs, high-end resorts and fitness equipment. In the closets of middle managers, the $40 Gap button-down gave way to the $130 Thomas Pink Oxford. Tickets for *The Producers* on Broadway starting at $100? Nursery school tuition for the twins rising to $16,000 each? Five bucks for a caramel macchiato? Cheap Money was a sticker-shock absorber.

Washington has always loved home ownership for purely pragmatic reasons: the Realtors, lenders, and home builders are powerful lobbies. But the new Republican majority believed the advent of an ownership society—more people owning assets like homes and stocks—would boost the GDP and the GOP. In his first term, President Bush and his allies reordered the tax code to favor investment income over wage income by cutting taxes on capital gains and dividends. However, these incentives did not have much effect. The percentage of households owning mutual funds fell from 49 percent in 2000 to 47.5 percent in 2005. That is not surprising, since you cannot buy mutual funds on margin. Bush was an aggressive promoter of financial assets one could acquire with debt. "Part of economic security is owning your own home," he said in 2002, in the home of an Atlanta-area police officer who had just bought a $130,000 town house with the help of a government loan.

The federal incentives promoting home ownership, which predated President George W. Bush, played an increasingly prominent role in the boom. The cost of the mortgage interest deduction, which subsidized big loans (the more you borrowed, the more you could deduct) grew sharply as housing prices rose, from $55 billion in 2000 to $66 billion in 2003. Fannie Mae and Freddie Mac, the progenitors of Network Finance, also acted as amplifiers. Their loan limits were tied to average home prices. So the more house prices rose, the more debt they would offer and insure. And the more they lent, the more prices rose. Between 2000 and 2004, a period in which real incomes fell, the conforming loan limit rose by nearly one third from 2000 to 2004, from $252,700 to $333,700.

Not everybody qualified for Fannie Mae and Freddie Mac mortgages. Buyers had to make down payments, show a certain credit score, and keep their loan amounts under the conforming limit. The need for housing credit thus gave rise to a new class of Cheap Money businesses: lightly regulated nonbank lenders who could borrow money in the capital markets, rather than from depositors, lend to whomever they saw fit, and then sell the mortgages as bonds. Foreign central banks might not buy the securities, since they lacked the implied guarantees of Fannie and Freddie debt, but other investors seeking higher yields in a period of historically low interest rates certainly would. Propelled by Network Finance, members of the Shadow Banking

sector began to emerge into daylight. Countrywide Financial
Corporation opened up storefronts all over the country, marketing cheap money. Fast-growing lenders like New Century Financial Corporation and Argent Mortgage targeted borrowers who
had heretofore remained outside the system. They pioneered
new technology that enabled more people to participate in the
market. In 2000, subprime was a tiny niche market, with the
719,000 loans outstanding representing about 2.4 percent of all
mortgages. But subprime origination rose from $210 billion in
2001 to $587 billion in 2004. These outfits also pitched adjust-
able-rate mortgages, which allowed investors to trade lower
short-term rates for long-term interest rate risk. ARMs (adjustable-rate mortgages), which accounted for 12 percent of mortgages sold in 2001, had a 19 percent market share in 2004.

Another prodigious borrower—the federal government—fol-
lowed a similar course. In the late 1990s, Alan Greenspan specu-
lated that the emerging government surpluses posed a danger to
the economy. In time, the government might pay down all its
debt and be forced to use surplus funds to buy stock in companies like, say, AIG and Citigroup. (At least he was half-right!) In
October 2001, at the onset of the Cheap Money era, Treasury
stopped issuing 30-year bonds, the most expensive form of financing, and tilted toward cheaper short-term debt. That turned
out to be a brilliant move. As President Bush and the Republican
Congress slashed taxes, increased domestic spending massively,
launched the new Medicare prescription drug entitlement, and
spent heavily on two wars, deficits soared. A $127 billion surplus
in fiscal 2001 turned into a $412 billion deficit in fiscal 2004.
The portion of the public debt held by the public rose from about
$3.4 trillion at the end of 2000 to $4.15 trillion in the first quarter of 2004—up more than 22 percent. But the taxpayers' interest
bill fell. In fiscal 1997, the first year of surplus, interest on the
public debt consumed $355 billion, or 22.1 percent of federal
outlays. But in fiscal 2004, interest costs fell to $322 billion,

amounting to only 16.5 percent of total layouts. Like home owners, the taxpayers were continually improving their cash flow
picture through refinancing. As old debt was retired, new debt
was issued at insanely low rates. In the spring of 2004, Treasury
could borrow for three months at an annual rate of about 0.9
percent, and for ten years at 3.625 percent. State and local governments experienced similar benefits. Their debt rose 33 percent from the end of 2000 through mid-2004, but the cost of
maintaining it held steady or fell. Even as New York City's debt
rose from $38 billion in 1999 to $48 billion in 2003, or 26 percent, the cost of carrying it fell sharply. Total funds spent on debt
service dropped from $3.74 billion in 1999 to $2.52 billion in
2003, from 10.4 percent to 5.7 percent of total expenditure,
thanks to sharply lower interest rates.

In fact, New York City, which had suffered such a devastating
blow on 9/11, was ground zero of the new Cheap Money economy. The new math and mentality surrounding debt and housing was a huge boon to the region's growth engine: Wall Street.

Lucrative initial public stock offerings fell off sharply in the
wake of the dotcom debacle, and New York attorney general
Eliot Spitzer was wreaking havoc on the investment banks' cozy
business models. Still, each piece of newly created debt—each
refinancing, each government bond issue—was money in the
bank for Manhattan. The volume of mortgage-backed securities
packaged and sold increased from $482.4 billion in 2000 to $2.14
trillion in 2003. Daily trading volume of mortgage-backed securities rose from $69.5 billion in 2000 to $211.5 billion in the
first quarter of 2004. The explosion created constant work for
bankers, lawyers, accountants, and printers. Further, each transaction threw off the lifeblood of Wall Street—fees: underwriting
fees for the big banks that packaged them, brokerage fees for the
investment banks that processed trades, and management fees
for the mutual funds and hedge funds that bought and traded
these assets.

The Era of Cheap Money created optimal conditions for the carry trade, the phenomenon whereby professional investors borrow cash short-term and buy higher-yielding long-term securities. When Greenspan slashed the federal funds rate to 1 percent in June 2003 and kept it there, banks could borrow short-term money for next to nothing and use the proceeds to buy a security like the 10-year Treasury bond, which yielded around 4 percent, or a Fannie Mae bond, which yielded a bit more. In its 2003 annual report, bond powerhouse Lehman Brothers noted that "principal transactions"—revenues from bets made with the firm's own capital—rose 119 percent in 2003, "principally reflecting record revenues from fixed-income products." Those who placed the bets won the internal sweepstakes. Lloyd Blankfein, an unassuming former gold-coin broker who headed Goldman Sachs's fixed-income unit, earned $20 million in 2003. His stewardship of the firm's new profit engine catapulted him to the posts of president and COO of the whole firm, and set him up as heir apparent to CEO Henry Paulson.

Cheap Money acted as both stimulant and balm. By 2004, jobs were growing, the stock market was rising, housing was booming, and partisans were declaring victory. In October 2003, radio host Jerry Bowyer published a book entitled *The Bush Boom: How a Misunderestimated President Fixed a Broken Economy*. The prosperity, however, was built on a vast increase in the amount Americans owe—collectively and as individuals. Total US nonfinancial debt—all the debt held by governments, households, and companies not in the financial sector—rose from $18.1 trillion in 2000 to $22.8 trillion in the first quarter of 2004. Total household debt went from $7 trillion at the end of 2000 to $9.5 trillion in the first quarter of 2004, up 36 percent. The amount of outstanding mortgage debt rose 43 percent in Bush's first term.

Since money was cheap, though, the cost of maintaining all this debt was manageable. Even as mortgage debt grew rapidly, the delinquency rate fell steadily, hovering around 2 percent through 2003 and 2004. Many companies that overborrowed to overinvest in the 1990s faced a reckoning in 2002—just as interest rates began to fall to new lows. "In 2002, companies that we thought were bankrupt pulled themselves together," said Steve Rattner, founder of the private equity firm Quadrangle Group. Defaults on corporate debt fell in 2003 and 2004 to 0.77 percent, according to Standard & Poor's. Despite the warnings of a few Cassandras, it was all good. And it would remain so as long as: (1) rates remained low; (2) asset prices continued to rise; (3) borrowers remained current on their payments; and (4) the markets for packaging and trading debt remained strong.

In the spring of 2004, the godfather of Cheap Money began to chip away at the first of these four pillars. Much as he would have wanted to, Greenspan could not keep short-term rates at the rock-bottom emergency rate indefinitely. (Some of us thought the emergency was that the incumbent Republican president was unpopular.) In the face of global growth and rising prices, and incipient signs of inflation, Greenspan returned to central banking orthodoxy. The June 30, 2004, decision to raise the federal funds rate from 1.00 percent to 1.25 percent signaled the beginning of the end for Cheap Money. However, it did not bring an end to the debt-fueled party. Not by a long shot. The mindset, technology, machinery, and incentives of free and easy credit had acquired lives of their own. Too many businesses, too many households, too many governments had become dependent on it. Greenspan may have thought he was taking away the punch bowl, but in fact, the party was just getting started.

CHAPTER IV

The Era of Dumb Money

The June 30, 2004, fed funds rate increase was perhaps the least surprising scrap of news to cross the tape since Nathan Lane came out of the closet. Investors fearful of revived inflation had pushed the yield on the 10-year Treasury bond from 3.65 percent in mid-March to 4.87 percent in mid-June—a spike of more than 30 percent. "The next ten years won't be like the last ten or twenty years," Columbia University economist Richard Clarida, a former assistant Treasury secretary in the Bush administration, told me. "There aren't going to be those big powerful forces pushing interest rates down." Through June 2006, the Fed, under Greenspan and his successor, Ben Bernanke, would raise interest rates seventeen times, jacking the fed funds rate up to 5.25 percent. Ten-year bond rates generally trended upwards, with fixed-rate mortgages following suit. The Era of Cheap Money was over.

In theory, the flattening of the yield curve should have put a brake on Cheap Money businesses like autos, housing, and Wall Street. Yet credit remained plentiful and relatively cheap in part because the Flat World Economics imbalances persisted. The trade deficit jumped to $712 billion in 2005, and commodities prices continued to rise. But something else was at work. The housing boom shed its skin to reveal the outlines of a housing credit bubble. And just as in the Era of Cheap Money, the new times required a new set of assumptions. "When the facts change, I change my mind," economist John Maynard Keynes said. When the facts surrounding debt changed, we did not change our minds. We changed our theories. Several factors—groupthink, hubris, and plain stupidity—combined to form a powerful Dumb Money cocktail. "Get stupid," blared the chorus from the Black Eyed Peas' 2004 party anthem. And stupid we got. The Era of Dumb Money was just beginning.

Cheap Money allowed home buyers to afford more expensive homes while insulating themselves from interest-rate risk, locking in guaranteed low rates for up to 30 years. But with both interest rates and home prices rising (up 12.4 percent in 2005 and another 4.1 percent through the first half of 2006), cheap money would increasingly come with a large potential cost. In February 2004, Alan Greenspan, momentarily morphing into CNBC personal-finance therapist Suze Orman, invited Americans to expose themselves to short-term interest-rate risk precisely at the time it would have been smartest to lock in a long-term rate. Headlining the Credit Union National Association's meeting—which also featured an actor "performing as the US Senator George Norris, original signer of the 1934 Federal Credit Union Act"—Greenspan explained that recent research found home owners could have saved tens of thousands of dollars had they held adjustable-rate mortgages (ARMs) rather than fixed-rate mortgages during the past decade. Duh! Interest rates adjusted only downward in that period.

When the oracle spoke, however, people listened. So instead of bargaining for lower home prices, we borrowed more, put less money down, and turned to innovative new products that offered reasonable initial payments. The volume of ARMs tripled between 2001 and 2004, from $304 billion to $985 billion. ARMs accounted for about 31 percent of the $2.9 trillion in mortgages issued in 2005. Funky new products like interest-only mortgages and option ARMs (which gave borrowers the option of not paying down principal, or only a portion of the interest) gained traction. In November 2005, Ownit Mortgage Solutions introduced a 45-year mortgage! If you were thirty and just beginning to nest, you would be committing to the same monthly payment until you were seventy-five. These so-called "affordability loans"—which gave buyers the illusion they could afford to buy a house at the market price—accounted for 25 percent of mortgage dollars lent in 2004 and 2005. In a normal market, an interest-only loan is tantamount to paying rent; the "home owner" builds no equity. Option ARMs are worse, offering the potential to build negative equity. But the logic of Dumb Money held that in a perpetually rising market blessed with perpetually low interest rates, both were painless paths to prosperity.

With the home ownership rate having crossed 69.2 percent in 2006, lenders exhausted the pool of creditworthy borrowers. And so mortgage brokers began to market subprime loans (made to people with poor credit scores) and Alt-A (or low documentation) loans with greater intensity. Subprime origination rose to $625 billion in 2005, up from $210 billion in 2001. Most of the big exotic mortgage specialists, like American Home Mortgage, a subprime lender founded in 1987 and based in Long Island that originated $5.4 billion of option ARMs in the 2006 third quarter, hailed from the Shadow Banking system. This new class of lenders defined itself as the customer-friendly, aggressive, helpful alternative to the local savings and loan. "When your bank says no, Champion says yes," as the ubiquitous ads for Champion Mortgage put it. Forget about jumping through hoops to meet the stringent standards of anal-retentive stuffed shirts. Faith-based shadow bankers made the same Dumb Money calculations that their customers did about home prices and interest rates. But they, along with old-style bankers who were hip to the new scene, like Washington Mutual, believed fervently in the new technology. Since Network Finance would permit them to sell off any risk associated with lending, they trusted without verifying, competed to lend to buyers, and profited by collecting fees.

The culture of subprime lenders was eerily reminiscent of the Silicon Alley/Silicon Valley lunacy of the late 1990s. In 2005, I worked briefly as a consultant for a company that was helping Argent, a subprime lender based in Irvine, California, start a magazine. Irvine, the planned community in real-estate mad Or-

ange County, was a hot spot of mortgage engineering. Subprime
lenders Ameriquest, Option One, and New Century were also
headquartered there. Now, in 2005, a decade into the digital age,
starting an expensive glossy magazine aimed at a group of people
who are not big readers did not strike me as a particularly smart
move. But Argent figured that producing a quarterly filled with
helpful closing hints and pictures of Danica Patrick, the brash
Indy car driver the company sponsored (splashy sports sponsor-
ships are another notorious sign of a market top), would encour-
age mortgage brokers to funnel business to the company. So we
ginned up articles on fixing credit reports, finding untapped markets for subprime—oops, nonprime—borrowers, like immigrants
(legal, preferably) and people who had just emerged from bankruptcy protection (they had no other debts and not many other
options). Part of the aim was to turn brokers into more coherent
versions of Alan Greenspan, able to translate Cheap Money theories about interest rates and ARMs into talking points.

Mortgage brokers, I learned, saw themselves as problem solv-
ers. And in the Era of Dumb Money, there was no financial problem a mortgage could not solve. In 2005's second quarter, the
delinquency rate for residential mortgages was 4.34 percent. Delinquency rates were substantially higher for ARM borrowers
(10 percent), while subprime fixed-rate borrowers turned in a
distinctly nonprime performance (9.06 percent). But, as Bill
Maher says, new rule! When people fell behind on their debts, it
was just another opportunity for fee-generating business. Mortgage brokers and lenders continually encouraged strapped borrowers to roll over their old mortgages into products that allowed
them to reduce payments but still "remain current." A borrower
in trouble could move from a 30-year fixed to a 40-year fixed,
then to an ARM, and then to an option ARM—continually trading short-term relief for greater long-term obligations.

Dumb Money was therefore self-sustaining—poor, untenable
housing-credit choices led inexorably to poorer, even more unten-

able options. But, as happens during bubbles, practices that later seem obviously absurd acquire their own logic. In the Era of Dumb Money, failure was simply not an option—for either borrowers or lenders. The foreclosure rate fell from 1.49 percent in the third quarter of 2002 to 1 percent in the second quarter of 2005. After the tiny Utah-based Bank of Ephraim went under in June 2004, 952 days would pass without a bank failure, breaking the 609-day record from the mid-1940s; 2005 was the first year since the FDIC's 1934 inception in which no banks failed. Government oversight, competitive pressures, and improved risk management played a role. However, Cheap Money and Network Finance played a bigger one. The yield curve was benevolent; securitization allowed banks to distribute risks from local loans to financial institutions around the world. "Under the recent economic conditions, it's been difficult to fail," FDIC chief economist Richard Brown told me in 2005. The lack of failure gave bankers an enormous amount of self-confidence; in tee ball, where it is impossible to strike out, everybody feels like a .400 hitter.

In every boom, there is a delicate moment when it becomes evident that the existing hot trends simply cannot continue. Throughout 2004 and 2005, there were abundant signs of unsustainability in the largest Cheap Money—and the first Dumb Money—business. At the end of 2004, US residential real estate was worth $18.6 trillion—more than the entire stock market. The National Association of Realtors reported that 23 percent of homes bought in 2004 were investment properties. In 2005, a record 8 percent of the nation's housing stock turned over. When Economy.com chief economist Mark Zandi created price-to-earnings ratios for housing (the rent a house could expect to bring in divided into its price), he found that the national P/E had risen from 9.3 in 2000 to 15 in 2005. In Las Vegas and West Palm Beach, the ratios were 121.3 and 120, respectively. (Factor in the inevitable maintenance and other costs of home ownership, and the ratios were even more out of whack.) Houses were the new tech stocks, valued not so much for the income they could produce as for their rapid growth potential. The S&P Homebuilders index soared from 201 in September 2001 to 1,323 in July 2005. In the fall of 2005, Miami real estate broker Mark Zilbert launched CondoFlip.com, a website where hotshots could flip $500,000 preconstruction condos in Miami the way day traders flip $15 stocks. Its motto: "Bubbles are for washtubs." Miami, a city with a population of 400,000 people and 70,000 condos in the works, was one big washtub. The frenzy triggered an outbreak of post-traumatic stress disorder among dotcom survivors. In March 2005, Merrill Lynch chief economist David Rosenberg con-structed twin charts showing that household real estate assets had hit 140 percent of GDP, the precise ratio that household mu-tual fund and stock assets had hit in 2000, just before the peak.

Unfortunately, Rosenberg was a Canadian-accented voice in the wilderness. Over and over again, we construct narratives to tell us why, if markets truly are efficient, numbers that seem so clearly out of whack are fine. Once the bubble is aloft, we take the delusion a step further, concluding that the recent party is a mere prelude to even greater revels. I call it Pro Forma disease. (Pro forma calculations, projections that rest on certain assump-tions, are a staple of MBA classes and business plans.) The main symptom is a compulsive tendency to extrapolate results of re-cent fat years endlessly into the future. The foolish book proph-esying Dow 36,000 did not come out in 1993 when the market was muddling along, but in 2000, after the Dow had tripled in seven years. Oil has spiked to $150? We have reached the point of peak oil, and the number of Chinese drivers is rising. Next stop: $200 per barrel. No one had a worse case of Pro Forma disease than David Lereah, chief economist at the National Association of Realtors. In February 2005, Lereah published *Are You Missing the Real Estate Boom?: The Boom Will Not Bust and Why Prop-erty Values Will Continue to Climb Through the End of the De-cade—And How to Profit from Them*. Real estate, he argued, was now in the midst of a permanent boom, fueled by demographics and the changes in the marketing and financing of homes. Never mind the impressive recent increases. Homes now represented a "once-in-every-other-generation opportunity." Robert Toll, CEO of McMansion giant Toll Brothers, was a fellow sufferer. In an October 16, 2005, *New York Times Magazine* cover story, he argued cogently that America stood on the precipice of a brave new world in which yuppies would soon pay half their incomes for mortgages and an average $1 million suburban home would go for $4 million. Absurd? Not if you engaged in a little Pro Forma thinking. Nationwide, mortgage payments on median-priced American homes ate up about 20 percent of income in 2005, according to Goldman Sachs. But in Los Angeles and New York, the ratios were 50 percent and 40 percent, respectively. "The company expects to grow by 20 percent for the next two years and then will strive for 15 percent annually after that," Toll said. That would mean a 66 percent increase in the number of McMansions completed in three years. But why not? Between 2002 and 2005, Toll's annual deliveries and revenues had essentially doubled.

Just as happened in the dotcom bubble, the bears, doomsayers, and buzzkills who warned that the economy had too many eggs in one basket, were marginalized. What did they know? As Harvard economist Jeffrey Frankel noted in May 2005, "Some of us have been warning of this hard-landing scenario for more than twenty years." And the killjoys were armed with mere data and history at a time when a new set of rules was in force. Consider the debate surrounding savings. In 2004, personal savings—which are computed by subtracting consumption from disposable personal income—were a scant $102 billion, less than 1 percent of GDP. The clear upshot: we should spend and borrow less, and squirrel more cash away. Optimists pointed out that the government measures of income used to calculate savings includes wages and salaries, interest on bonds, and stock dividends but excludes capital gains on stocks, profits from selling a house, or withdrawals from 401(k) plans. That did not seem right in a society where half of households owned stocks and roughly the same percentage was flipping condos in Las Vegas. "The structure of the household portfolio has changed over time," said David Malpass, chief economist at Bear Stearns, one of the leading exponents of what might be dubbed the Theory of Magical Market Savings, the notion that speculative behavior can be an important, recurring source of savings. In 2004, Malpass found that, thanks to the booming stock and housing markets, the net worth of US households—their assets minus their liabilities—stood at a record $48.54 trillion, up 9.6 percent from 2003; in 2005, the measure rose another 5.2 percent to $51.1 trillion. When rising markets do the heavy lifting of savings, we should not fret about the number of nickels deposited in piggy banks. Of course, this too was a strain of Pro Forma disease. The Magical Market Savings Theory made sense as a national strategy only if asset prices moved in only one direction. It is difficult for a bank, or a mattress, to take away your savings. However, it is quite easy for Mr. Market to do so.

Alas, in the Era of Dumb Money, daydream believers who thought their houses were functioning as asset-accumulation accounts woke up each morning to find their faith rewarded. Incomes were stagnating, but consumption continued to rise, because the Shadow Banking system and Network Finance allowed home owners to monetize paper gains. The amount of HELOCs outstanding rose from $714.8 billion in the first quarter of 2004, and $917.25 billion in the first quarter of 2005. Mortgage equity withdrawal continued to soar, to $915 billion in 2005. In 2004 and 2005, "Personal expenditures in the past fifteen months have been largely financed by borrowing," Cambridge economist Wynne Godley noted in May 2005. "Even a reduction in the pace of debt creation will force people to start spending less, on a big scale."

In the Dumb Money Era, debt was widely rebranded as leverage—not a burden but a powerful force that lets you lift more than you could otherwise. And the trend toward using leverage to boost home purchases and consumption worked its way up the income ladder. James Grant, editor of *Grant's Interest Rate Observer*, noted with alarm an advertisement in the *Wall Street Journal* for interest-only loans with a negative-amortization option available for up to $5 million. Who could afford a $5 million house but not have sufficient cash to keep up with monthly payments? "The rich who happen not to have money," he concluded. A survey by the Spectrem Group, an anthropologist of the well-to-do, found 14 percent of people with more than $5 million in assets had credit card balances. (Maybe John McCain, with his eight houses and large American Express balances, was not such an aberration.) The ultrarich-only luxury emporium Neiman Marcus was the subject of a fevered auction in May 2005. One of its crown jewels was the in-house credit card unit, which had some 562,000 active users, and about $550 million in receivables—about one-sixth of the company's 2004 sales was bought on layaway, by people paying 15 percent interest.

A second important bubble-era mode of thinking came into play during the Era of Dumb Money. In virtually every bubble, players adopt a mind-set that new technologies grant users superhuman powers to master economic vicissitudes. In the 1850s, executives believed the telegraph would be the perfect demand-management tool and thus could help smooth out the occasionally vicious business cycle. Consultants peddling customer relations management software said the same thing about the internet in the 1990s. Of course, technology is—and has always been—a tool, not a panacea. And frequently it simply allows humans to justify bad decisions or to impose their poor judgment across a broad system instantaneously. In this period, Wall Street came to believe that securitization and derivatives could manage and even banish the most complicated and unpredictable forms of risk. Aside from creating and issuing mortgage-backed securities (MBS), Fannie Mae and Freddie Mac also bought and sold MBS, and derivatives based on those securities, in an effort to hedge their risks. These were effectively giant fixed-income hedge funds. Despite that, the two firms convinced themselves and investors (they had a combined market capitalization of well over $100 billion in 2005) that massive exposure to interest-rate volatility can be a low-risk business, that a giant financial company, through efficient hedgings, can produce earnings as smooth and predictable as those reported by General Electric in Jack Welch's heyday.

Other components of the Shadow Banking system reached the same conclusion. As Cheap Money gave way to Dumb Money, the Smart Money crowd—Wall Street banks—hit upon a few realizations. With the yield curve flattening, the practice of borrowing short and lending long ceased to be highly profitable. They saw that a new class of clients—hedge funds—were doing quite well trading with leverage. And so, like real estate brokers who realized they could make more money flipping condos than collecting commissions, large investment banks decided they would rather be principals than mere agents. The more debt they could use—raised from the capital markets, not depositors—the more juice they could get out of good trading and investment ideas. There was a catch. The Securities and Exchange Commission, which had an interest in brokerage firms remaining solvent, required broker dealers to maintain one dollar of capital for every twelve dollars of debt they held.

In the spring of 2004, Wall Street's establishment investment banks—Goldman Sachs, Merrill Lynch, Lehman Brothers, Bear Stearns, and Morgan Stanley—successfully appealed to the SEC to waive the rules. (Among those petitioning was Goldman CEO Henry Paulson.) Funds held in reserve, they argued, could be liberated to invest in mortgage-backed securities and derivatives. Oh, and the brokers could use computer models to gauge the riskiness and value of the new types of securities they would buy. SEC commissioner Roel Campos said he supported the change with his "fingers crossed." To convince investors and lenders that the business model made sense, the Five Horsemen of the Dumb Money Apocalypse began to introduce new terms into the debate. Technology enabled them to quantify precisely how much they could lose if things went wrong, how much of the firm's—and hence investors'—capital was at risk every day. VAR—Value at Risk—became a staple of quarterly and annual reports. Lehman Brothers assured investors in 2006 that the firm, which had hundreds of billions in mostly short-term debt outstanding, could lose no more than the $42 million on an off day.

Of course, for Shadow Banks like Lehman, which lacked a base of insured depositors, access to capital would turn out to be a sometime thing. An episode involving one of those rich borrowers provided an early tremor for the monster earthquake of 2008. Refco seemed to be the ultimate Smart Money play. It was a broker, a fee-generating middleman nicely positioned in booming commodity and capital markets. Thomas H. Lee, the highly respected private equity investor, took a big stake in the company in the summer of 2004. The following August, gold-plated underwriters Goldman Sachs and Credit Suisse First Boston brought it public, raising $583 million. But on Monday, October 10, 2005, it was reported that an entity controlled by Refco CEO Phillip Bennett had owed $430 million to the company, as part of an effort to hide trading losses. The revelation changed nothing material in Refco's financial situation. Bennett paid the money back—apparently, he had a spare few hundred million lying around—and quit the same day, and the company hired squeaky clean former SEC chairman Arthur Levitt to clean things up. But Refco's business was facilitating trades conducted essentially through a digital handshake. Companies like this rely on liquidity—the ability to access vast stores of credit instantaneously and cheaply—and on the willingness of other institutions to wait a day or two before receiving payment. Once the trouble was announced, Refco's customers began to yank funds and steer business elsewhere. Starved of liquidity, Refco collapsed within a week; $4 billion in market capitalization vaporized. In abandoning Refco so rapidly, the market proved that for Shadow Banks, creditworthiness is not an absolute attribute, but something you have to earn every day.

As previously discussed, this new, new economy rested on four pillars: perpetually low rates, perpetually rising asset prices, borrowers remaining current on payment, and strong markets for packaging and trading debt. In 2004, the first pillar started to crumble. By 2006, after another eighteen months of rising speculation and mortgage innovations, the imbalances that built up during the Era of Dumb Money caused the second and third pillars to develop some cracks. Even the most optimistic economists could not escape the laws of supply and demand. By the spring of 2006, as increasing numbers of developers and house flippers stricken with Pro Forma disease entered the fray, nearly 4 million homes were for sale. That was about twice the inventory of 2000. By June 2006, the month in which the housing market peaked, thanks to high prices and low standards, 6.2 percent of subprime loans were in foreclosure or arrears. But these data points were easily written off. The failures were the marginal players. On July 20, Ben Bernanke told Congress, "The downturn in the housing market so far appears to be orderly." And whatever problems existed seemed to be confined to the housing market.

If only. By the middle of 2006, the virus of bad lending and the scourge of Pro Forma disease were spreading from housing to Wall Street and to corporate America at large. The ethos of Dumb Money was migrating from the bottom-feeders—subprime lenders—to the aristocrats of the financial services industry: investment banks, private equity firms, and hedge funds. The Smart Money crowd would prove the avatars of a period of even Dumber Money.

CHAPTER V

The Era of
Dumber Money

In ordinary times, a bursting housing bubble would have hurt home builders, real estate agents, and regional banks holding mortgages. But the wholly predictable (yet somehow entirely unexpected) housing decline would have deeper, global implications, thanks to Network Finance. And Wall Street's go-go culture would push the credit bubble into two dangerous new directions *after* the housing market peaked. First, like teenagers moving on from relatively safe "gateway" drugs to the harder stuff, the Shadow Banking system devised new, dangerous ways of using mortgage debt. Second, the same enabling assumptions and technology behind Dumb Money, which had turned a mortgage from a 30-year relationship between two consenting parties into a zipless f*** involving dozens of players, began to influence the burgeoning *corporate* credit market. As the bad-lending virus spread from housing into the rest of the economy, a new class of Cheap Money players—hedge funds and private equity firms—began to act like bubble-era home buyers. Finance imitated art, if the Farrelly Brothers' movie *Dumb and Dumber* is your idea of art. For in many ways—grand historical irony alert!—the Smartest Money would prove to be dumber than Dumb Money.

The subprime problems that cropped up in 2006 were easily dismissed. Conventional wisdom held that these mopes were the finance industry's used-car salesmen—cheesy outsiders with déclassé customers. But Wall Street's golden boys, the investors and firms lauded in *Barron's* for their superior investing acumen, plunged deeply into subprime lending *after* the housing bubble had reached its peak. The youthful, highly regarded hedge fund manager David Einhorn in 2006 built a significant position in New Century, the huge subprime lender, and joined the company's board of directors—just in time to watch the stock turn into a bagel. In July 2005, ex–Goldman Sachs wunderkind Dinakar Singh and the huge private equity firm Texas Pacific Group teamed up to invest $100 million in mortgage exotica pioneer ResMAE (it pitched a 30-year mortgage that borrowers could pay as if it amortized over 50 years). On February 13, 2007, ResMAE broke investors' hearts by filing for Chapter 11.

During the Era of Dumber Money, large, old-line investment banks waded chest-deep into the subprime swamp. They provided credit to the likes of Argent and New Century, and then bought the raw material from these lenders, which they packaged into mortgage-backed securities. Between 2003 and 2006, nonagency mortgage-related debt issuance more than doubled, from $345 billion to $773 billion. The dynamics of the market had shifted. In 2003, Fannie Mae, Freddie Mac, and other agencies issued eight times more mortgage-related bonds than Shadow Bankers did; in 2006, the ratio fell to 1.6:1. The Shadow Bankers lent the process a more dignified, industrial air by dubbing their undertaking Structured Finance. In the grips of Pro Forma disease, and a malady psychologists have dubbed Compulsive Fee-Seeking Disorder, Wall Street knew that there was big money to be made processing the debt—bundling it, selling its pieces, and helping others trade them.

As competition for the raw material rose, banks were forced to offer higher prices for mortgages of lower quality. In the 1890s, John D. Rockefeller's Standard Oil pursued a strategy of vertical integration, the better to ensure the availability of commodities at prices it could control. Standard ultimately did everything from producing crude oil to owning gas stations. The twenty-first-century investment banks looked back to the nineteenth century for inspiration. Under the leadership of CEO Stanley O'Neal, a child of the segregated South who in 2002 became the first African American to head a major Wall Street brokerage, the largest investment bank, Merrill Lynch, plunged into the business of packaging mortgages. To ensure a steady supply, Mother Merrill adopted some of the industry's problem children. In 2005, Merrill took a 20 percent stake in Ownit Mortgage Solutions, purveyor of the 45-year mortgages, and then lent it money. When Ownit (it should have been called Owe-It) went bust in December 2006, Merrill was its largest unsecured creditor. In September 2006, long after cracks appeared in the subprime market, Merrill paid $1.3 billion for subprime lender First Franklin Financial Corporation. Under the leadership of John Mack, Morgan Stanley, the least subprime of Wall Street's biggest firms, spent $706 million to acquire Saxon Capital, the fourteenth-largest subprime lender, in August of 2006. All these deals were horribly mistimed. But thanks in part to the presence of these large players, speculative lending continued well after the housing market peaked. Historically, mortgage lenders had required borrowers to make down payments of at least 10 percent. In 2007, according to the National Association of Realtors, 45 percent of first-time home buyers put no money down, and the median first-time home buyer financed a massive 98 percent of the purchase. In a declining market, these practices were recipes for rapid losses.

There was a second reason Wall Street wanted to control the raw material. The innovation in how mortgages were made was accompanied by great innovation in the way mortgages were packaged, sold, and traded. The big banks were not simply manufacturing mortgage-backed securities. Rather, they began forming MBS into collateralized debt obligations (CDOs). CDOs, which would join KKK and PLO as notorious three-letter acronyms, started off as a relatively benign form of derivative. Think about the way that seafood restaurants chop up clams into strips, bellies, and whole clams for people with different budgets and tastes. An investment bank like Merrill could buy a pool of subprime mortgages, which carry interest rates of, say, 9 percent, and then slice them up. The top chunk, or tranche, would have the first claim on interest paid into the pool. And since those would get paid off even if some mortgages might fail, that slice would be deemed a safer investment, and hence would yield about 6 percent. A wedge in the middle might yield 9 percent, and the slice at the bottom, the last in line to get paid, might pay 12 percent. Each of these tradable tranches was rated by a credit rating agency according to its risk profile. The volume of CDO issuance rose from $157 billion in 2003 to $552 billion in 2006, with Merrill leading the way.

In theory, CDOs were risky—the promoters had no idea what would happen if something went wrong. But the ratings agencies—Standard & Poor's, Moody's, or Fitch—happily slapped ratings on them in exchange for the mother's milk of Wall Street: fees. As one Standard & Poor's analyst wrote in an internal 2007 email: "We rate every deal. It could be structured by cows and we would rate it." (See what I mean by Dumber Money?) But if you were a believer in the one true faith of Cheap Money, this business was, um, udderly brilliant. Financial alchemy could turn subprime straw into prime gold.

Even if a CDO did go bad, a second component of the new financial technology would come to the rescue: derivatives. New derivatives were constantly being created. In August 2006, the Chicago Mercantile Exchange, working with a company founded by Robert Shiller, the Yale economist, introduced futures and options on housing prices in ten cities. Few home owners used these derivatives, which offered the type of beneficial insurance that Shiller had long advocated. No, the Smart Money crowd would use another kind of derivative: credit default swaps (CDS).

If structured financial products were the new industrial products—like machinery or bridges or buildings—they could be insured. Starting in the 1990s, bankers at J.P. Morgan pioneered the

CDS. CDS allowed members of the Shadow Banking system to buy and sell insurance policies on financial assets—corporate bonds, mortgage-backed securities, or even CDOs. They were bilateral deals, with one party agreeing to pay the second party in the event a third party defaulted on its debt. CDS, like CDOs, could also be traded. Bankers compared the origins of the CDS market to the Manhattan Project. As one J.P. Morgan banker told *Newsweek*, "There was the same kind of feeling of being present at the creation of something incredibly important." There must be a secret room in Harvard Business School where irony is vaporized from the brains of MBAs. For in time, the analogy to the origins of the nuclear bomb would prove all too apt.

Lehman Brothers was a large dealer of CDS. However, AIG Financial Products, a small unit of the insurer AIG and member of the Dow Jones Industrial Average, became the market leader, writing policies on trillions of dollars of debt in exchange for small annual premiums. The prices it set were based on a proprietary model developed by Yale economist Gary Gorton. But in practice, this was another Dumb Money pro forma business. CDS issuers sold insurance at cheap rates because they did not think the insured companies would default; after all, defaults on corporate debt had been very low in recent years, falling to 0.76 percent in 2006, according to New York University debt expert Ed Altman. A hedge fund could borrow money to buy high-yield bonds that yielded, say, 10 percent, and then hedge its bets by purchasing a cheap credit default swap. By using CDS, members of the Shadow Banking system were, in effect, putting themselves on the hook for trillions in payouts if things went badly. The amount of debt insured through CDS rose from $100 billion in 2000 to $6.4 trillion in 2004, and then achieved fission in the Era of Dumber Money, rising to $62 trillion by 2007.

Consider for a minute how the humble mortgage had evolved. In the 1990s, it was a simple contract between two parties, executed to allow a person to buy the house he or she would live in, and made to be held. In 2006 and 2007, a mortgage was likely made to help finance consumption or a speculative home purchase, then turned into an MBS, which could be held and traded by several parties, then molded further into a CDO, which would be traded by still others, which in turn could become a product on which other investors could write CDS. It was like a wedding cake: debt layered on debt, frosted with debt, gilded with sugary debt obligations, and topped with a bride and groom made of (you guessed it) debt. All this innovation did not create much value, save for the fees it produced. "Nobody needed a CDO," as the senior executive at a large investment bank told me. And the vibe was less high-technology than Dr. Seuss. In *Yertle the Turtle*, the burp of the humblest terrapin could bring down the whole tower. Given the structure that had been erected, the failure of a single mortgage could affect a whole range of assets piled on top of it. In an age when financial failure simply was not an option, few people thought through the new technology's implications.

The beauty of this technology was that it could be applied to other areas, creating new opportunities for Wall Street fees. In early 2005, Marvel Entertainment CEO Avi Arad stood in Paramount's Sherry Lansing Theater and pitched a group of Wall Street executives on the idea of lending him more than $500 million, putting up Captain America and Nick Fury and the Avengers as collateral. "I don't know who was in the audience, but I think there was a lot of money in there," Arad told me. There was. In the fall of 2005, Marvel rolled out a $525 million debt facility to finance the production of up to ten big-budget ($165 million a pop) live-action films based on comics characters. With Wall Street firms like Merrill Lynch and Credit Suisse First Boston acting as matchmakers, Marvel, Disney, and Warner Bros. linked up with private equity investors. "A few years ago, we began to see huge demand for US-dollar investments from Asian investors in particular," said Michael Blum, the low-key head of global asset–based finance at Merrill Lynch. And so movies were turned into structured financial products, the better to soak up excess global savings. If bonds can be backed by pools of mortgage payments, why couldn't they be backed by box office receipts and DVD sales of a studio's production slate? "With multiple revenue streams generated by the film, there's more potential cash to pay down the debt," said Jay Eisbruck, managing director at the credit-rating agency Moody's, which gave its blessing to these deals. "Also, when the whole slate is being securitized, successful films can offset the failure of others." In 2004, Paramount created Melrose Partners, which raised $231 million to fund 20 percent of the production costs of every film. Merrill Lynch sliced and diced Melrose into three types of pieces: high-yielding debt and equity for hedge funds, and lower-yielding debt for banks—and sold them in $5 million chunks. The fund backed films such as *Mean Girls* and *War of the Worlds*. Network Finance meets Hollywood!

Hedge funds and private equity, the big dogs of the Shadow Banking system and the driving force of the Era of Dumber Money, lapped up the innovatively structured products. In 2006 and 2007, the mentality that informed the Dumb Money on housing and housing-related credit shifted to other sectors. And much of the new debt created by the Shadow Banking sector was used to fund the activities of private equity firms like the Carlyle Group, Kohlberg, Kravis & Roberts (KKR), the Blackstone Group, and Apollo Management.

With their English airs—wood-paneled offices filled with oil paintings, antiques, plush carpets, and secretaries with impeccable British accents—the private equity firms were the aristocrats of Wall Street. Indeed, superprime big shots like Henry Kravis and Stephen Schwarzman seemed the polar opposites of subprime hustlers. But the analogies between the alpha and the omega of the financial world were obvious and numerous. First, as had been the case with housing debt, Cheap Money pushed banks into willful disarmament. Historically, most bank loans

came loaded with covenants—early-warning systems that stipu-
late that the borrower has to keep spending to a certain level or
keep the ratio of debt under a certain amount. But as private equity firms started to do larger deals, banks competed for their
business by lowering standards. Starting in 2005, Wall Street
banks began extending "covenant-lite" loans. Blissfully free of
such requirements, these were the equivalent of low-document
home loans. In May 2007, according to Goldman Sachs, such
loans accounted for 15 percent of outstanding bank debt.

Later in the housing bubble, option ARMs emerged as a dangerous alternative to a fixed-rate mortgage. The corporate analog
was payment-in-kind (PIK) notes, bond issues in which borrowers
either can pay interest in cash, or, if they don't feel like doing
that, they can "pay" with more debt. Those started to appear in
the spring of 2005, and over the next three and a half years, dozens of companies, virtually all of them backed by private equity
firms, would issue nearly $38 billion in PIK notes. Private equity
firms were heavy users of what might be called Henny Young-
man finance. (Take my money. Please!) Freescale Semiconductor,
the large technology firm taken private in 2006 for $16.5 billion
by a group of private equity players—the Blackstone Group, Per-
mira Funds, the Carlyle Group, and TPG (Texas Pacific Group)—
in November 2006 issued $1.5 billion of PIK notes.

There's more. In the Era of Dumb Money, people took out
HELOCs and regarded them as savings and income. In the Era of
Dumber Money, financiers did something quite similar. A firm
like Blackstone or Apollo Investment would use primarily debt
to buy a company with a pretty decent balance sheet. Then the
owner would have the company issue more bonds—maybe PIK
notes— and use the proceeds to pay a juicy dividend to the new
owners. Voilà! They could generate instant returns, not through
improving operations or implementing a new business strategy,
but through financial engineering. The practice was dubbed
"dividend recapitalization," though it was the functional equiv-

alent of mortgage equity withdrawal. Apollo bought Verso Paper for $1.4 billion in 2006, using $290 million of its own cash and $1.1 billion of newly issued debt. In 2007, Verso used some of the cash raised through that debt to pay its new owners a $250 million special dividend.

Dumb and Dumber Money led to larger and larger deals. Fifteen billion dollars for Hertz in November 2005, $16.5 billion for Freescale Semiconductor, $27.4 billion for Harrah's Entertainment, $33 billion for HCA (Hospital Corporation of America), and $45 billion for Texas utility TXU in February 2007, finally surpassing the legendary R. J. Reynolds–Nabisco deal of 1989. Nine of the ten largest leveraged buyouts in history were announced between July 2006 and July 2007. According to investment-technology specialist Dealogic, the volume of buyouts rose from $395 billion in 2003 to $790 billion in 2006 and $1.13 trillion in 2007. Investment and commercial banks were lulled into a false sense of security, just as they had been with the FDIC's record of days without bank failures. Advisory fees (for "advice" that generally consisted of saying, "Hey, great idea, Henry!" and printing up some cool deal gifts) were significant. "Greed has taken over," Carlyle Group cofounder David Rubenstein said at an industry conference in May 2007. "Nobody fears failure." No company seemed too big to elude the reach of the new Mr. Bigs. So as the Dow pierced 13,000 and then 14,000, scaling new heights, a new wrinkle of Dumb Money thinking was used to justify the rising asset prices. Remember the Greenspan put? In the Era of Dumber Money, pros began to speak of a private equity put. The notion that private equity players could come in with an offer to buy control of a company, no matter how large, helped raise the floor beneath stocks.

In the Era of Dumber Money, the financial system reversed Shakespeare's admonition. Everybody a borrower or a lender wanted to be. Established banks were carpet bombing downtowns with outlets. In my hometown of Westport, Connecticut, population 25,000, there were 26 branches. The number of new banks formed rose from 91 in 2002 to 178 in 2006. Between 2004 and 2007, 630 banks were started. But the branchless banks—the Shadow Bankers—were providing most of the new credit. "Many of the entities that created so much credit in this cycle are not subject to capital or reporting requirements at all," said Roger Altman, CEO of investment bank Evercore Partners. "And many of the very exotic financial instruments which represented extreme leverage don't carry minimum capital requirements." Indeed, rather than act as brakes, the biggest institutions with the biggest balance sheets (and hence the most to lose from reckless lending) acted as accelerators.

Blame it on two powerful forces: the power of pro forma thinking and the culture of Wall Street. If, say, a banker at Lehman Brothers had stood up and said that subprime lending was a disaster, that the Cheap Money/Dumb Money thinking could wind up destroying the firm, he would have been gently shushed. Pulling back would have been like unilateral disarmament. Every CDO that Merrill Lynch would not underwrite was one that Morgan Stanley would. In late 2006, Mike Gelband, the executive at Lehman Brothers in charge of residential and commercial real estate, told senior management that the rising prices and lowering standards made him nervous. "We have to rethink our business model," he said, according to Steve Fishman's excellent *New York* magazine postmortem on Lehman. But Gelband was dismissed as a wuss. "You don't want to take risk," CEO Richard Fuld told him. A few months later, Gelband was out. (He was rehired by Lehman in June 2008.)

In the Era of Dumber Money, the grown-ups were not quite in control. No bank was a bigger player in the world of easy corporate debt than Citigroup. Its CEO, Charles Prince, was promoted in 2003 to clean up after the 1990s bender and rationalize far-flung operations. Investors thought that Prince, a creature of the conference room rather than the trading floor, would bring a culture of sobriety and careful management of risk. But just as Merrill pushed into subprime mortgages and CDOs under Stanley O'Neal, Citigroup similarly rushed into the erogenous zone of private equity lending, even after it was clear things had gone a bit too far. In the summer of 2007, as deals were getting bigger and loan terms easier, the executive formerly known as Prince famously described the 195-year-old bank's strategy thusly: "As long as the music is playing, you've got to get up and dance. We're still dancing." As long as the market was demanding it, a force the size of Citi, with its $2 trillion balance sheet, believed it had no choice but to keep making loan commitments. Citi ultimately extended $114 billion in what became known as "leveraged loans" to back private equity deals.

If the practice sounds dumb, the theory was sound. Network Finance and technology would spare banks any ill effects. Loans were sold off in chunks or could be pooled into CDOs. Signed syndicated credit facilities by US borrowers rose from $129 billion in the first quarter of 2005 to $332 billion in the second quarter of 2007, the height of the Dumber Money Era. And those buying the pieces of the loan could insure themselves against loss by purchasing credit default swaps. Through 2007, it was all working beautifully. In May 2007, I sat in the office of Andy Serwer, the managing editor of *Fortune,* who was reviewing a long piece on the outlook for corporate America. The thesis? "Dead calm," he said. Things had never been better for the Fortune 500 and especially for Wall Street. Hedge funds were generating gigantic commissions through furious trading of all sorts of assets. Debt issuance was rocking. In 2006, Lehman Brothers reported that its fixed-income capital markets revenues increased 15 percent to $8.4 billion. Buyouts were booming. That year, Morgan Stanley advised on $977.2 billion of announced mergers and acquisitions—nearly $1 trillion!—more than three times the 2004 total. At Goldman—a huge, highly profitable hedge fund lashed to a huge, highly profitable investment bank—the "principal strategies business" in 2006 generated $13.23 billion in profits, up from $6.2 billion in 2004. With each passing quarter, it put more of its investors' capital at risk. The average value at risk was $101 million for the 12 months ended in November 2006.

The operating assumption of all these businesses—Citi with its private equity loans, Merrill with its CDOs, Goldman with its proprietary trading desks, private equity firms with their financial engineering—rested on a deep, debt-fueled market, the fourth pillar of the Dumb Money faith. The technology supporting Network Finance worked only so long as there were willing buyers and traders. If you assembled subprime mortgages to make a CDO but could not sell the pieces, you would be stuck holding a lot of them. If you extended credit for a $30 billion private equity deal and could not syndicate the loans, you would be stuck with it. But the faith in the new technology was so strong that the thought did not crop up. There was always out there a Greater Fool—a hedge fund, another bank, a sovereign wealth fund, a rich Arab or European—who was searching for a yield-producing asset. The housing market may have peaked, but Wall Street, and the nation at large, were punch-drunk on the numbers posted in the Era of Dumber Money. And we began to see the classic signs of the late stages of a bubble: truly dangerous self-confidence among leading players and evidence that a financial phenomenon was crossing over into the larger culture.

CHAPTER VI

Hedge Fund Nation

In the last, degenerative stage of a bubble, the phenomenon always jumps the shark. Surfers who have prospered by riding the waves believe they can walk on water and take the trend to ludicrous extremes. The energy and enthusiasm crosses the fortified borders separating the financial realm from the political and cultural worlds. The investment craze, once limited to first-moving professional investors, is pitched to second-, third-, and fourth-moving amateurs. More people pile on, desperate not to miss out. That is what happened in the age of Dumber Money in 2006 and 2007, the prelude to the inevitable pop. If this were the Roman Empire, the Era of Dumber Money would be the reign of Caligula.

Hedge funds and private equity firms were holding a nonstop jam session, playing the music that got Citigroup's Chuck Prince up on the floor and boogeying. Success and debt combined to transform the new industries into huge, increasingly irresistible forces. According to a splashy October 2007 McKinsey report on the rising class of new financial power brokers—hedge funds, private equity firms, sovereign wealth funds, and emerging markets—assets of hedge funds rose from $625 billion (in 4,598 funds) in 2002 to nearly $1.7 trillion (in about 7,000 funds) in the first quarter of 2007. Drawing a line forward—consultants have a genetic susceptibility to Pro Forma disease—McKinsey suggested hedge funds' assets could rise to $3.5 trillion by 2012. Private equity funds' assets under management rose from $323 billion in 2000 to $709 billion in 2006. In 2006 alone, US private equity firms raised $179 billion. The borders between hedge funds and private equity firms, two peas in the Dumber Money pod, began to erode. Blackstone, a private equity fund, opened hedge funds, and hedge funds like Cerberus Capital Management, which had started life trading distressed bonds, began taking ownership of entire companies.

For this new crowd of big swinging dicks, the ability to borrow vast sums of money functioned as powerful implants. More impressive than the size of their deals was the income they produced. For all their storied histories, mission statements, and vast global footprints, investment banks like Lehman Brothers and Merrill Lynch were essentially conduits for compensation. A typical Wall Street firm pays 50 percent or more of its revenues in salaries and bonuses. But hedge funds and private equity funds paid out virtually all their revenues as compensation, which made them the envy of their financial services brethren. Hedge fund and private equity managers get a small management fee—1 percent or 2 percent of assets under management—plus 20 percent of investment profits. A $1-billion fund up 20 percent for the year throws off $20 million to spend on overhead and $40 million in incentive fees to distribute to employees. Since it does not cost much more to manage $1 billion than it does to manage $100 million, larger funds were even more profitable. And funds that were really good, like the quantitative Renaissance Technologies hedge fund, could keep an even larger chunk of the profits.

Of course, there was a fundamental flaw in this model. Given the management and incentive fees, hedge funds would have to do really well to justify their pay. In a year that the S&P 500 rose 10 percent, a hedge fund's investments would have to rise about 15 percent to make investors believe they were getting solid after-fee results. And just as there are not 8,500 market-beating mutual fund managers, there are not 7,000 market-beating hedge fund managers. Of course, unlike mutual fund managers, hedge fund and private equity operators could magnify returns by borrowing. And so in the age of Dumber Money, leverage and rising markets turned hedge funds into ATMs. In 2007, the top fifty individual hedge fund managers made $29 billion, and the top five made $12.6 billion, which, as author Matt Miller notes, "was equal to the combined pay of the lowest-earning nine million workers." And here's the kicker. The incentive fee, known as carried interest, money paid for managing other people's money, is taxed as capital gains rather than as ordinary income. Instead of paying the top rate of 36 percent on seven-figure payouts, hedge fund and private equity dudes (they were almost all men) paid a mere 15 percent to Uncle Sam. The industries' twin Washington lobbies—the Managed Funds Association and the Private Equity Council—managed to beat back the flurry of outrage that erupted in the summer of 2007 when Congress discovered the carried-interest wrinkle.

In part due to increased lobbying, the air traffic lanes between New York and Washington were clogged with the private jets of the new industrial statesmen. As with dotcom entrepreneurs and tech company CEOs in the 1990s, politicians sought out hedge fund and private equity managers—for their counsel, for their considered opinions on all manner of policy, and for their campaign donations. Cheap Money and Dumb Money had elevated stock slingers and merchants of debts to Wise Men, new archetypes of success. And none more so than Stephen Schwarzman, cofounder of the Blackstone Group. Having conquered the world of private equity, Schwarzman wanted to be seen as *un homme sérieux*, in the image of Averell Harriman (whom he had met when he was a Yale undergrad) all while continuing to do bigger and bigger deals. Schwarzman, who was described to me by a longtime associate as "a talented consumer," acquired the trappings of a Rockefeller Republican, including an apartment on Park Avenue once owned by John D. Rockefeller Jr., and was tabbed as chairman of the John F. Kennedy Center for the Performing Arts in Washington. In a 2004 *New York Times* interview, he mused about how he might like to be the next Treasury secretary. But when it came time for President Bush to replace John Snow, who quickly found a job with Cerberus Capital, Bush chose another Ivy League–pedigreed banker who had been turned into a genius by Dumb Money: Goldman Sachs CEO Henry Paulson. Schwarzman consoled himself by throwing a $3 million birthday party at the Park Avenue Armory in February 2007, with Rod Stewart and Patti LaBelle as entertainment.

The immense profits that accrued to those who skillfully deployed Cheap Money altered the social geography of New York. Private equity and hedge fund managers threw themselves, and their new money, not just into parties, but also into politics, education reform, and charity. The annual gala of the Robin Hood Foundation, founded by Paul Tudor Jones II, became an occasion for conspicuous earners and conspicuous consumers to become conspicuous donors. The 2006 event raised $48 million. And the tendency of hedge funds to congregate in prestigious buildings in both Upper Hedgistan (Greenwich, Connecticut) and Lower Hedgistan (midtown Manhattan, especially on Park Avenue and around 57th Street) caused rents to spike to more than $100 per square foot in both hot zones. That had the effect of encouraging pro forma thinking among landlords. My office at *Newsweek* sits in an older, shabbily genteel building on the corner of 57th and Broadway, in which *Newsweek* had for nearly a decade occupied several high floors with excellent views of Central Park. In 2007, the building's owner, the Moinian Group, decided to renovate the building, sheathe it in glass, rename it 3 Columbus Circle, boot out existing tenants, and jack up rents by a factor of seven. After all, by the spring of 2009, when *Newsweek* was slated to leave, hedge funds would be falling over themselves to pay top dollar for the digs. Wouldn't they?

In the latter stages of most bubbles, people from outside the hot industry—including many who never showed much interest in business at all—always plunge headfirst into the boiling waters. Remember the Fortune 500 corporate warriors who rein-vented themselves as dotcom hipsters in the spring of 2000? In January 2007, former chairman of the Securities and Exchange Commission Richard Breeden—a man who, as Lynnley Brown-ing of the *New York Times* wrote, "has no investing experience"— became a hedge fund manager, complete with a $500 million start-up pile, a Cayman Islands registry, and an office in Green-wich. The same month, Clinton's secretary of state, Madeleine Albright, announced the formation of an emerging-markets hedge fund. Albright Capital Management was backed with $329 million in seed money from PGGM, a Dutch pension.

Hedge funds and private equity were no longer exotic and ex-clusive, but an easily understandable and necessary asset class. Yale endowment chief David Swensen had racked up impressive returns for nearly two decades by eschewing liquid bonds for il-liquid alternative investments like private equity, hedge funds, and commodities. Swensen became the hot new guru for endow-ments and other nonprofits, which began to follow the Yale model. Asset management companies, especially publicly held investment banks, began to market hedge funds, previously available only to the ultrarich, to the merely rich. And why not? It was a hell of a lot more exciting than collecting deposits from civil servants and making small business loans or running index funds. Having captured the businesses of mining and processing of mortgage debt, the Shadow Banks now wanted to capture the money to be made from managing structured financial products. In April 2007, Citigroup bought Old Lane, a hedge fund created by former Morgan Stanley executive Vikram Pandit, for more than $800 million. Goldman Sachs, which had long done well trading its money, started in-house bond hedge funds like the $1.8 billion Liquidity Partners, in the summer of 2007. Bear Stearns, which operated with about $30 of debt for every dollar of capital, started the Bear Stearns High-Grade Structured Credit Strategies Enhanced Leverage Fund. In addition to using every

Dumb Money buzzword, the fund used debt to buy mortgage-backed bonds. These moves represented either another step toward vertical integration or the addition of another layer of debt onto a multitiered cake.

Next, individual investors—the kind who could not afford to have their money managed by Goldman Sachs—were ushered past the velvet ropes. In February 2007, Fortress Investment Group, a nine-year-old hedge fund complex with about $30 billion under management, became the first hedge fund manager to go public. Its shares priced at $18.50 and closed the first day at $31, a 67.6 percent increase, making the stakes of Fortress's five founders worth a combined $9.4 billion on that day. But there was something strange about the whole deal. These expert traders, the sort of people who always seemed to know something the rest of the market did not, were selling. And if hedge funds were so expert at funneling cash to their owners, why were Fortress's owners suddenly willing to share ownership with you and me? A few months later, the first major private equity firm went public. Blackstone, with $80 billion under management, raised $4.13 billion in an initial public offering and used much of that cash to buy shares from existing shareholders like Schwarzman and Peter G. Peterson. "Blackstone Group is a very, very, very bad deal for investors," wrote Jim Jubak of MSN, "though one that I expect to be hugely popular anyway." It was. On the first day of trading, June 21, 2007, Blackstone's shares, initially priced at $31, rose to $38 and closed at about $35.

Next came publicly held hedge funds. In July 2007, the Carlyle Group, a leading private equity firm, rolled out Carlyle Capital Corporation, whose business model was to borrow oodles of money—up to $32 for every dollar of cash it had—and buy things like mortgage-backed securities. In short order, Carlyle Capital would deploy $670 million to control $32 billion of mortgage-backed bonds. What, you may ask, is the difference between this fund, and, say, a home buyer who buys a house with 3 percent down? Not much. In either case, a 3 percent decline in assets would wipe out all the equity. Instead of relying on a 30-year mortgage to back the purchases, Carlyle Capital relied on short-term loans from banks. KKR, the snobbish private equity pioneer, in 2005 staged an initial public offering of KKR Financial Holdings at $24 a share. KKR Financial had the same basic idea as Carlyle Capital, borrowing money to buy securities, but it kept its leverage to a more modest 9 to 1.

Until 2006 or 2007, private equity had been a thinking man's game. Align the interests of ownership and management, fix the underlying business, and use debt both as a tool for lifting and for imposing discipline on managers. Leveraged buyouts had been the equivalent of using a mortgage to purchase a house, giving the contractors a piece of the ownership, and spending a few years fixing up the joint before selling it. Companies, like homes, were chosen for their solid foundations that could support the new loads. McKinsey's sanguine 2007 report noted, "Private equity tends to invest in relatively stable companies, limiting the effects of economic downturns on their performance and enabling companies to finance higher levels of debt." Well, increasingly in the Era of Dumber Money, *Not!* Drunk on Dumb Money, and on their own success, financial operators and their lenders threw the old rules out the window—just as home owners and mortgage companies had done in 2005 and 2006. The financial engineers came to believe that because they had made a lot of money flipping assets with cheap credit, they could apply their genius to industries in which they had little expertise. Stock pickers were instantly reinvented as retail geniuses, hedge fund managers as industrial saviors, and real estate barons as new media gurus.

In 2003, the brilliant hedge fund manager Edward Lampert, who had been tagged as the Warren Buffett of his generation, acquired Kmart out of bankruptcy and used it as a platform to buy Sears in 2005, creating a 3,800-store behemoth that occupied a dubious place in the retail firmament whose lodestars were mass affluence and trading up. Lampert did not do much to fix Sears and Kmart's lame merchandising and tired stores. Capital investment shrank, and so did same-store sales—down 5.3 percent in 2005, 3.7 percent in 2006, and 4.3 percent in 2007. In May 2007, Lampert acknowledged the importance of same-store sales but noted, "They're not the be-all and end-all." Bizarrely, the fact that he appeared almost indifferent to the nuances of retailing seemed to be a plus. The stock soared fifteenfold, from $13 in May 2003 to $192 in April 2007, largely because investors believed he would perform some of that Dumb Money hoodoo. If Sears failed as a retailer, investors reasoned, Lampert could liberate the value of the firm's real estate or sell off stores to other deep-pocketed buyers. Best of all, he could use cash generated from operations to run it like a publicly traded hedge fund. In reality, Lampert used the excess cash to buy back stock, which is a genius move in a rising market but a dunce move in a falling one. Between the third quarter of 2005 and the end of July 2008, Sears would buy back 38.7 million shares at a total cost of $4.8 billion, an average price of about $124 per share.

In the fall of 2007 came a more extreme example of the Dumber Money axiom that no domain knowledge was necessary. Sam Zell, the Chicago-based real estate investor, nicknamed the Grave Dancer for his delight in picking up dead businesses and reviving them, had lashed together a collection of high-end office buildings to form Equity Office Properties Trust. In February 2007, he unloaded the company in an all-cash transaction valued at about $38 billion to the Blackstone Group, which put in $6.4 billion in cash and borrowed the rest in one of the last huge private equity takeouts consummated. And lo, verily, Dumb Money begat Dumber Money. Blackstone flipped a bunch of the buildings for a big profit almost instantly. And Zell decided that good timing in flipping real estate made him an expert on the ailing newspaper industry. In April 2007, Zell announced he would spend $8.2 billion to acquire of the Tribune Company, which owned the *Los Angeles Times*, the *Chicago Tribune*, and the Chicago Cubs. Zell put down a mere 4 percent of the purchase price—$315 million—and borrowed much of the rest. The Tribune Company deal, which closed in December 2007, was a classic Dumb Money play. Zell did not have much of a strategy for reversing the revenue decline at the newspapers. He loaded up the company with nearly $13 billion in debt, which would require interest payments of nearly $500 million in the first half of 2008. But so what? Citigroup, Merrill Lynch, and Morgan Stanley feasted on the advisory and underwriting fees associated with the deal. The plan, such as it was, was to pay down debt not with operating cash but with sales of Dumb Money assets—trophy properties such as the Chicago Cubs, office buildings, and big-city newspapers whose purchase would require easy credit. Those sales, of course, would generate even more fees.

From Dumb (Sears), to Dumber (Tribune), to Dumbest. If there was one industry on which you could not rely for cash flow to pay off big fixed debts, it was newspapers—or maybe CD sales. Yet British private equity firm Terra Firma in August 2007 paid $4.8 billion, most of it borrowed, to buy EMI, the record company whose revenues were shrinking rapidly. To win this dubious prize, EMI had to beat out another Latin-themed player, Cerberus, which had just pulled off a Dumber Money perfecta. In April 2006, Cerberus acquired 51 percent of GMAC, the auto financing unit of General Motors that had branched out into home lending—a Cheap Money business squared. Then in May 2007, Cerberus bought 80 percent of Chrysler from Daimler for $7.4 billion. Cerberus believed it could limit risk by selling off pieces of the deal to other private equity and hedge funds, fix operations, improve the carmaker's finances, sell it a few years down the road, and be hailed as an industrial savior. While private equity was no panacea, John Snow, the former Treasury Secretary who had become a top executive at Cerberus, told the National Press Club in July 2007, "In certain cases like Chrysler, we believe it offers simply the best hope for restoring competitiveness to sectors of the US economy that need it most."

By the middle of 2007, iconic brands such as Sears, Jeep, Harrah's, Hilton, and GMAC had been subsumed into Hedge Fund Nation. This trend was just a sign of a larger, more ominous development. Mainstream old-media companies, with their long-term corporate-planning processes and general lack of urgency, are frequently clueless about business and slow to learn about new trends—and even slower to capitalize on them. Which makes them perfect top callers. In the summer of 1929, John J. Raskob, a former auto executive, wrote an article in *Ladies' Home Journal* that urged everyday Americans to build leveraged portfolios. It was a clear tremor of the impending crash. *Time* made Amazon.com's founder, Jeff Bezos, Man of the Year in December 1999, and *Fortune* put Krispy Kreme on its cover in July 2003, right when the doughnut maker hit its peak.

Hedge funds began to saturate popular culture in the Era of Dumber Money. In the fall of 2006, *Hedge Funds for Dummies* was published, and Kenneth Cole unveiled a $160 pair of loafers called the Hedge Fund. In June 2006, I attended previews for an off-Broadway play about hedge funds. (And no, it was not *Katz*.) *Burleigh Grime$* revolved around the romanto-comic antics of a rogue hedge fund manager, a Maria Bartiromo-esque television reporter he uses, and a junior employee who seeks to gain familial revenge. It starred Mark Moses of *Desperate Housewives* and Wendie Malick of *Just Shoot Me* (which, oddly, is what I said to the person sitting next to me during intermission). Imagine a David Mamet play without humor, irony, or incisive thoughts—in other words, two hours of cursing. In October 2006, Doug Ellin, who developed *Entourage* for HBO, started work on an HBO series based on . . . a hedge fund. In May 2007, when buzzy television shows like *Dirty Sexy Money* and *Gossip Girl* were glorifying the New York money culture, the *New York Times* reported that Fox had greenlighted a sequel to the classic 1987 film *Wall Street*, in which Michael Douglas would reprise his role as Gordon Gekko. Working title: *Money Never Sleeps*.

Hedge Fund Nation was particularly evident in the media most likely to be behind the times—print. Magazines that chronicled the life and work of hedge fund studs, like *Trader* and *Alpha*, grew as fat as the *Industry Standard* in 1998. Dana Vachon, who had worked at J.P. Morgan, made his bid to be a modern-day Jay McInerney with his spring 2007 novel, *Mergers & Acquisitions*. The narrator of the Dumb Money chronicle, based loosely on Vachon, is Tommy Quinn, "the worst young investment banker on Wall Street." And in April 2007, the most anticipated article in the most anticipated magazine launch was Tom Wolfe's takedown of the carried-interest crowd in the debut issue of Condé Nast's *Portfolio*. Twenty years after *The Bonfire of the Vanities*, Wolfe chronicled how a new pack of interlopers—"hedge fund managers . . . private equity fund managers . . . stock and bond traders, and various lone-wolf entrepreneurs such as real estate developers" with their vile manners, bad taste, unforgivably cheesy clothes, and even worse diction—were laying waste to all that was good and sacred, while redefining New York's commercial culture and social life.

All parties end, of course. Just as the November 1987 publication of *The Bonfire of the Vanities* neatly coincided with the stock market crash, Wolfe's exposé of the Dumb Money titans came out just in time. The dismay Wolfe felt over their rise was laced with envy and anger at the way these guys had used debt as a social and cultural booster rocket. But perhaps it could have been leavened with a little *schadenfreude*. As those ad-thickened issues of *Portfolio* were going to press, the edifice of Dumber Money was already starting to crumble. When I checked prices online in the spring of 2007, Kenneth Cole's Hedge Fund loafers were marked down 25 percent. That was a portent of things to come.

CHAPTER VII

The Slow Unmasking

By mid-2007, the glitzy Hedge Fund Nation patina could no longer mask the rot in the house of Dumb Money. Interest rates were increasingly unpredictable, asset prices were falling, borrowers were falling behind, and the technology behind the boom—the markets for securitizing debt and derivatives—began to experience intermittent crashes. "History has not dealt kindly with protracted periods of narrow risk premiums, meaning excessive risk taking," Alan Greenspan told me in an October 2007 interview. "Euphorias come out at the end with debacles." But the intellectual architects of the era, who had spun glorious tales about the savings glut and the brilliance of securitization, were constitutionally unable to recognize the spreading crisis. They chalked up the growing list of small collapses to poor execution rather than to shabby design. Even as more people were hobbled by the lethal virus of bad lending, our public financial health officials declared it quarantined. Again and again. The failure was as much one of imagination as of management. Nobody in a position of responsibility could imagine that things would get bad. And when things got bad, nobody could imagine they would get worse.

Housing prices had fallen for twelve straight months between August 2006 and July 2007, a source of great befuddlement to the pundits. "Most of the correction in home prices is behind us, but general gains in value next year will be modest by historical standards," David Lereah, the Baghdad Bob of real estate, said in his December 2006 forecast. Existing-home sales would fall 1 percent to 6.4 million in 2007, with prices rising 1 percent. Oh well. In 2007, existing-home sales fell 12.8 percent, and prices *dropped* 6 percent. Toll Brothers, whose CEO in 2005 had forecast 15 percent growth endlessly into the future, in 2007 delivered 26.5 percent *fewer* homes than it did in 2005.

Similarly, the greatest economic minds of our era missed the broader turn in housing and housing credit. On October 9, 2006, Greenspan declared, "The worst may be over for housing." In March 2007, Treasury secretary Henry Paulson told the House of Representatives that "from the standpoint of the overall economy, my bottom line is we're watching it closely, but it appears to be contained." Two months later, Federal Reserve chairman Ben Bernanke assured the public that "we do not expect significant spillovers from the subprime market to the rest of the economy or to the financial system." By the summer, however, he estimated the losses due to subprime debt would be "in the order of between $50 billion and $100 billion."

Had Bernanke lifted his eyes from his prepared remarks, he could have seen significant spillovers. For the last pillar of Dumb Money—the deep, wide, and efficient market for the trading of securitized debt assets of all types—was crumbling. Bear Stearns had always been the pesky, uncouth runt of the Wall Street family. In June 2007, two large hedge funds run by its asset management unit, including the High-Grade Structured Credit Strategies Enhanced Leverage Fund, ran into trouble. The funds had borrowed heavily to invest in CDOs, whose value fell as delinquency rates on subprime mortgages rose. To protect itself, one of the fund's lenders, Merrill Lynch, seized $850 million of the fund's assets that had been posted as collateral. However—in a harbinger of the cluelessness to come—Merrill had a hard time getting a good price for them. Bear Stearns did other banks and the rest of the market a solid by agreeing to bail out one of the funds (and its many creditors). Crisis contained.

This rush to declare the spills contained—again and again—is a typical postbubble reaction. For the belief in the story of the hot industry frequently persists even after the markets have peaked. Any break in a frothy, irrational market presents a once-in-a-lifetime buying opportunity. Amazon.com at $400 might be a bit too rich for your blood. But at $150? Strong buy! This mentality was one of the two Dumb Money forces driving the huge surge in foreclosures. According to RealtyTrac, the number of foreclosure filings—default notices, auction sale notices, and bank repossessions—rose from about 885,000 in 2005 to 1.26 million in 2006, up 42 percent. The foreclosure filing rate nearly doubled from September 2006 to September 2007. People who bought homes with no money down had nothing to lose by walking away. At the same time, banks and investors believed they had everything to gain by foreclosing quickly. Let's say a lender had made a 100 percent loan on a condo in Irvine, California, for $600,000, and the borrower defaulted with $590,000 in principal remaining. In the Era of Dumb Money, when prices moved in only one direction, the bank or an investor who acquired the loan could foreclose, put the condo back on the market, and sell it for $650,000—instant profit. In October 2007, Henry Paulson noted, "Recent surveys have shown that as many as 50 percent of the borrowers who have gone into foreclosure never had a prior discussion with a mortgage counselor or their servicer."

By the summer of 2007, it should have been obvious that mass foreclosure sales would add large chunks of supply at precisely the wrong time, especially in bubbly markets like Las Vegas. However, factors unique to housing and Dumb Money guaranteed the reckoning would be deliberate. After bubbles pop, markets go through a painful process in which participants try to agree on prices for formerly inflated assets. A stock can go from $60 to $0 in a matter of days. But, contra the speculation-driven CondoFlip.com, houses cannot be flipped like stocks. People live in their homes, and there are big transaction costs associated with selling them. The amount of debt involved created powerful incentives for all players to delay rapid price discovery. Home owners did not want to mark down the value of their homes 20 percent overnight, because it would make it impossible to pay back mortgages if they had to sell and would limit their ability to refinance or take out home equity loans. The banks did not want to concede that houses had fallen suddenly in value, because it would require them to boost reserves against potential losses, and so on down the line to bondholders and the firms that insured structured financial products. The presence of massive debt thus acted as a brake. Between October 2006 and October 2007, according to the Case-Shiller index, housing prices fell only 6.1 percent.

Given that so many homes had been bought with little or no down payment, even these modest declines meant bad news for mortgage lenders and traders. And as they began to falter, the Smart Money crowd sensed once-in-a-lifetime bargains. When Countrywide Financial, the largest mortgage lender, saw its stock fall by half in the first eight months of 2007, Bank of America, which did a lot of business with Countrywide, plowed $2 billion into the company in the form of an interest-bearing security that could be converted into common stock at $18 per share. By the end of the year, Countrywide's stock fell into the single digits. In September 2007, Joseph Lewis, one of Britain's wealthiest men, spent $680 million on a 7 percent stake in Bear Stearns, whose stock had fallen after the hedge fund debacle, paying an average of about $107 per share, according to the *Wall Street Journal*. Other firms, not believing the Dumb Money era had ended, simply refused to accept lifelines. In April 2007, WCI Communities, the builder of "amenity rich" condos in Florida that began to falter in early 2007, dismissed a $22-per-share takeover offer from vulture investor Carl Icahn as inadequate.

To a large extent, the Dumb Money economy had become the whole economy. Cars, the biggest retail sector, were utterly dependent on cheap credit. In an age of stagnant wages, mortgage equity withdrawal had become a key support for sustaining consumer spending. The financial sector's share of total US corporate profits rose to a massive 35 percent in 2007. And yet economists, who had done so much to make the world safe for Dumb Money, seemed constitutionally unable to recognize that things were coming undone. In the best of times, economists are poor prognosticators. "I've been forecasting for fifty years, and I had not seen any improvement in our capability of forecasting," Greenspan told me. But the dismal scientists, who suffer from Pro Forma disease, are particularly bad when it comes to inflection points. *The Economist* reported that in March 2001—the month in which a recession began—95 percent of American economists thought there would not be a recession. Christina Romer, the Berkeley economist who is now a key economic adviser to President Obama, said economists could not predict recessions and economic discontinuities because they are inherently unpredictable. Almost all the postwar recessions were preceded by a shock, like a spike in short-term interest rates or a sharp rise in oil prices. "It's impossible to see the shocks coming," she told me.

Executives were not of much help, either. In contrast to the dotcom boom, the Era of Dumb Money was largely the construct of men in their fifties and sixties who had lived through plenty of economic cycles. They had risen through large institutions and had run them quite well, in fact, as evidenced by their lofty stock prices. Dumb Money acted like helium, inflating egos and reputations. In Hedge Fund Nation, intelligence was measured exclusively by net worth. We had great faith in the capabilities of the CEOs of Lehman Brothers and the Blackstone Group. Cheap Money and a rising market had turned them into superheroes, blessed with foresight, courage, and perfect knowledge.

In the fall of 2007, I went to see the Wizard. A colleague and I were ushered into a nondescript office in Dupont Circle for an audience with Alan Greenspan. In a two-hour conversation, I was simultaneously impressed with his brilliant exposition of the last two decades of monetary policy and somewhat troubled by the undergraduate-level philosophy lessons he dispensed about the nature of man—views that plainly informed his world-view on interest rates and regulation. One of the chief architects of this new financial structure, with its profligate use of debt, possessed a zealot's belief in the power of technology and had an abstract fervor for the glories and potentials of creative destruction. Several weeks later, I was seated near John Thain, the CEO of the New York Stock Exchange, at a luncheon. When he mentioned that he did not watch CNN—too biased!—and got his television news primarily from Fox News Channel, I nodded politely and almost fell out of my chair. Here was the head of the world's most important securities exchange, a graduate of MIT who had risen to a top post at worldly Goldman Sachs, and who, within months, would be anointed the savior of Merrill Lynch. (Within a year, it would turn out that Thain was a better decorator than manager.) And he had the news consumption habits of a dittohead? The world had generally regarded Treasury secretary Henry Paulson as a genius because he had amassed a $500 million fortune while rising to the top of Goldman Sachs. Yet his public speaking style was halting, unconfident. During a January 2008 interview in his baronial office in Washington, DC, I asked for some perspective on recent events and received little more than Cheap Money maxims. I left with a sense that, like many of the investment bankers who cobbled together Dumb Money deals, Paulson was great at grappling with the assignment on his desk and not so great at thinking through the implications. Toward the end of our visit, I noted that to that point, Goldman Sachs seemed to have dodged the bullets that had injured many Wall Street firms and asked if Paulson had any insights as to why. "Goldman did pretty darn good when I was running it, too," he said, rising and moving on to his next task. Of course, there were signs that even Goldman was vulnerable. In the fall of 2007, one of the hedge funds it managed blew up, and Goldman had to bail it out with $2 billion of its own money.

The ebbing credibility of the top players—this Slow Unmasking—ultimately would prove to be extremely corrosive. Credit, which comes from the Latin meaning "belief," is above all a confidence game. Shadow Banking and Network Finance rested entirely on the willingness of investors to extend credit to one another, to go to sleep at night knowing that Lehman Brothers or Bear Stearns could handle several hundred billion dollars of debt. And in the fall of 2007, belief was in increasingly short supply, thanks in large measure to a chronic inability to diagnose the problems of bad credit. When Merrill Lynch reported second-quarter earnings on July 17, chief financial officer Jeff Edwards said the firm's exposure to subprime was "limited, contained, and appropriate." On October 5, twelve weeks later, Merrill announced that "challenging credit market conditions" would cause it to take write-downs of $4.5 billion on subprime mortgages and other debt instruments. On July 20, Citigroup CEO Charles Prince crowed about record earnings generated by its panoply of Dumb Money businesses. On October 1, when Citigroup said it would have to take nearly $5 billion in write-downs because of the credit catastrophe, Prince assured suddenly nervous investors that "we expect to return to a normal earnings environment in the fourth quarter." It was as if they had all received shots of Botox; they seemed to wear expressions of perpetual surprise. Prince was out of a job five weeks later. By the fall, when the mortgage problems began to go global—Swiss giant UBS said that problems "mainly related to deteriorating conditions in the US subprime residential mortgage market" would force it to take a $3.4-billion loss and suffer its first quarterly loss in nine years—respected market watchers were tabbing the system's collective subprime losses at between $250 billion and $500 billion. But in congressional testimony in November, Bernanke would go only so far as to say that estimates of losses up to $150 billion were "in the ballpark" and reassured us that the problems were contained. If the Cold War containment policy had worked as well as this subprime-mess-containment policy, we would all be speaking Russian and living on collective farms.

After denying the trauma for so long, many participants began to move on to the second stage of grief: bargaining. Yes, there were some problems, but it was nothing a little Cheap Money could not cure. Bernanke had boosted the federal funds rate to 5.25 percent in 2006, to ward off a potential spurt in inflation. In August, as the credit markets seized up, CNBC's Jim Cramer had a now-famous on-air meltdown. "My people [Dumb Money types] have been in this game for twenty-five years. And they are losing their jobs, and these firms are going to go out of business," he screamed. He begged Bernanke for cheaper money. Robert Nardelli, the CEO of Chrysler, the highly leveraged private equity play whose sales depended on free and easy credit, echoed the call. Martin Wolf, chief economics commentator of the *Financial Times*, formed an international auxiliary, appealing to America's Dumb Money self-image. "The US has been the world's spender and borrower of last resort," he wrote. Cutting interest rates would allow Americans to resume their selfless acts of good global citizenship.

Bernanke responded and began cutting rates in September. But the Fed controlled only the rates at which banks borrowed from the Fed. The Shadow Banking system determined the rates at which home owners, Wall Street banks, and private equity firms could borrow. And as the secondary market for funky debt began to seize up, vertical integration, which had allowed Shadow Banks to reap big profits, became a liability. For Citigroup and Merrill Lynch, the faltering market was a double-edged sword: they could no longer profit by selling bonds backed by mortgages or other debt, and they had to keep the stuff on their books and recognize losses as the value of the debt fell. On October 5, several weeks after promising a return to profitability, Kerry Killinger, then CEO of Washington Mutual, a bank that never met a borrower it did not like, said, "a weakening housing market and disruptions in the secondary market" would cause net income to fall by hundreds of millions of dollars in the third quarter.

The secondary market for bank loans and corporate bonds was suffering as well. Throughout the first half of 2007, private equity firms continued to make ever-larger deals. In June, a consortium struck a $48.5-billion deal to acquire Canadian telecommunications company BCE. However, by the fall banks found it difficult to sell the debt they had committed to raise for these deals. In August, banks were sitting on up to $400 billion of debt to finance megadeals. At the end of the third quarter, Merrill Lynch had $31 billion in leveraged loans waiting to be sold, and Citigroup had $57 billion. As lenders pulled back, deals began to fall apart, and the stock of deal makers like the Blackstone Group started to droop. A vicious new malady—Erect Deal Dysfunction—began afflicting middle-aged men who lived on the Upper East Side. Suddenly, they could no longer consummate mutually satisfying transactions with eager partners.

As 2007 drew to a close, the virus of bad debt had become an epidemic. The delinquency rates for all sorts of debt—prime mortgages, auto loans, student loans, and credit cards—began to rise. At first, the Shadow Banking system mobilized to bail itself out. Private equity firms started funds to buy the discounted bank debt committed to leveraged loans. Large investment banks bailed out customers of busted hedge funds and other investment vehicles. When the investment banks started to run low on cash, they turned to Sovereign Wealth Funds. In December, Citigroup raised $7.5 billion from the Abu Dhabi Investment Authority, and Merrill Lynch raised $4.4 billion from Singapore's Temasek Holdings.

From Washington came muted *Horton Hears a Who!* suggestions that banks take more aggressive actions. In the fall of 2007, Sheila Bair, chairwoman of the Federal Deposit Insurance Corporation, urged banks to systematically modify loans by, for example, converting teaser rates into permanent fixed-rate loans.

They should do so, Bair argued, not out of charity or civic-mind-edness, but out of self-preservation. "It was clear that foreclosed homes going on the market was putting additional downward pressure on home prices—and was leading to a spiral," as she put it. In the fall, Henry Paulson and his colleagues suggested the creation of an industry coalition, Hope Now, to coordinate mod-ification efforts. However, thanks to the complications of Net-work Finance, there were few takers. "We've got this great complexity, where the investors are scattered around the world, and that makes decision making very complicated," Paulson told me in January 2008.

And so as 2008 opened, despite a series of embarrassing stum-bles, the mask was only half off. The economy had done what it had always done—absorb and process failure quickly and move on. Housing and its related industries might have been past their prime, but there were new sources of dynamism, such as alterna-tive energy, commodities, and exports. Economists surveyed by the Philadelphia Federal Reserve in November 2007 forecast that the economy would grow 2.5 percent in 2008, and add 103,500 jobs per month. And the problems with housing and credit had been contained. The National Association of Realtors projected existing-home sales would rise ever so slightly to 5.7 million and that the median home price should rise 0.3 percent. "Now that mortgage conditions have improved, some postponed activity should turn up in existing-home sales over the next couple of months, and I expect sales at fairly stable to slightly higher lev-els," said Lawrence Yun, who had replaced David Lereah as NAR's resident cockeyed optimist. (*Plus ça change.*)

But the slow unmasking had changed some things. The World Economic Forum in Davos convened in late January just as the Dumb Money crisis was revealed to be contained to a new area. In response to revelations that a rogue trader at French bank BNP racked up $7.1 billion in trading losses, global markets began to gyrate wildly. Several investment bank CEOs, reluctant to leave

their turrets, canceled or shortened their visits. Sovereign Wealth
Funds were the new belles of the ball. On one panel, the crowd
strained to hear every word uttered by representatives of funds
from the Persian Gulf and Norway, while Blackstone's Stephen
Schwarzman sat on the end, practically ignored. Doomsayer
Nouriel Roubini, whose dire premonitions had rendered him a
quasi-outcast in previous years, was exalted as a seer. Hedge fund
manager George Soros hosted an I-told-you-so lunch for journalists—veal, as I recall—at which he blamed much of the debacle
on George W. Bush and warned of worse to come. Indian and
Chinese bureaucrats, economists, and CEOs chastised the US for
its subprime problems, while assuring the audience—and themselves—that their own remarkable growth would continue un-
abated. (How, I wondered, do you say "Pro Forma disease" in
Mandarin?)

It was easy for the fortunate global citizens enjoying Davos's
toasty mix of proximity to power and abundant free food and
drink to chortle at the misfortunes of others: the subprime borrowers and foolish lenders, the suddenly humbled private equity
magnates and bankers. But as was the case with the Thai buffet
at Davos—oddly accompanied by a mariachi band—we had all,
especially the Americans, been eating from the same contami-
nated all-you-can-eat Dumb Money trough. And in 2008, we
would all get really, really sick. Having run out of Greater Fools
on which to offload risk, the Shadow Banking system would find
a new class of fools with infinitely deep pockets: American taxpayers.

CHAPTER VIII

The Great Unwinding

Leverage was like an elaborate pulley system that allowed us all—from the humblest consumer to the most exalted private equity baron—to hoist a mammoth weight. But in 2008, the rigging broke. The large weight plummeted, propelled by the twin forces of mass and gravity, flattened the balsa-wood fortifications of Dumb Money and Cheap Money, and left a giant hole the American taxpayer had to fill in. Hedge Fund Nation quickly transformed into Bailout Nation. As the Slow Unmasking of 2007 gave way to the Great Unwinding of 2008, the weak assumptions supporting Dumb Money stopped making sense. Suddenly there was no global savings glut providing endless supplies of cheap capital for Americans; no market magic sparing consumers the tough slog of saving money; no shock-absorbing power in securitization and derivatives.

In many ways, the economy entered uncharted territory in 2008. We know how stocks perform at different points in economic cycles. But even the sharpest number crunchers had no inkling of how large quantities of credit default swaps would be settled or how rising default rates on subprime debt would affect the valuation of CDO tranches. (The answer: badly.) To a degree, the continual, total failure of those responsible to gauge the severity of the crisis was understandable. The financial world had changed so much that forecasting was like projecting the impact of a grid-wide power shutdown in 2008 based on experience from the failure of a single, isolated power station in 1892.

In early 2008, it became apparent that the market alone could not deal with the emerging problems. Bear Stearns fell out of favor in the summer of 2007 when two of its hedge funds blew up. In the ensuing months, investors became increasingly concerned about its high level of debt, repeated losses, and the fact that its seventy-something CEO, James Cayne, seemed to spend a lot of time playing golf, competing in bridge tournaments, and, according to the *Wall Street Journal*, sparking up the odd doober. In February and March 2008, Bear Stearns's stock spiraled downward. Despite the removal of the unable Cayne and Bear's repeated protestations of solvency, the market ignored Journey's anthem: it stopped believing. And as Bear faced the prospect of bankruptcy in mid-March, the federal financial bureaucracy finally sprang into action. Treasury secretary Henry Paulson hammered out a deal for JPMorgan Chase to access credit from the Federal Reserve to buy the investment bank at a bargain-basement price of $2 per share (later revised upward to $10 a share). The response was, by definition, hastily improvised. When commercial banks failed, a tried-and-tested procedure kicked in: the Federal Deposit Insurance Corporation took charge and made insured depositors whole. But there was no protocol for how to deal with a huge, highly networked investment bank. Because of its massive levels of debt and the crucial position that it held in the markets for credit default swaps—in other words, because of this Shadow Bank's centrality to Network Finance—Bear Stearns had the capacity to harm hundreds of financial institutions.

While the crisis was contained, once again, a sense that something was not quite right lingered. "You have this whole synthetic economy created with derivatives and swaps, and it's like the sorcerer's apprentice," said Felix Rohatyn, the Wall Street *éminence grise* who was an adviser to Lehman Brothers. Yet he was sanguine about the place where he hung his hat. "Dick Fuld, who is the chairman of Lehman, had to take the firm through the cataracts here, and the leadership overall in dealing with this crisis has been quite good." Economist Mark Zandi, who had been prophetic about the links between housing and the larger economy, said that Washington had woken from its slumber. "Congress and more prominently the administration seem to be moving toward a more aggressive response toward the housing and mortgage crisis," he said. The collapse, he suggested, might be a "cathartic event in that it forces policy makers to act more aggressively." Alas, over the next nine months, Wall Street would stage more cathartic events than a Greek drama festival.

By the summer, each of the four pillars of Dumb Money had crumbled. Despite the projections of growth, jobs and housing prices fell in every month, which meant the dynamics underlying debt continued to weaken. And it was not just housing. *All* the Dumb Money asset classes—mortgage-backed securities, CDOs, the stocks of private equity and hedge funds, bank debt sold to finance bailouts—began to fall. Values fell in part because borrowers were not staying current. In April, the percentage of mortgage borrowers behind on their payments—6.35 percent—was the highest since the Mortgage Bankers Association began tracking the number in 1979. In the first quarter of 2008, 36 percent of all foreclosures initiated were on *prime* adjustable-rate mortgages in California. The rising tide of debt spurred lenders to demand greater returns. And so while the Federal Reserve sharply lowered the short-term interest rates it controlled, long-term rates failed to follow suit. Rates on jumbo mortgages, corporate bonds, and the loans banks make to one another spiked, sometimes sharply. Banks acted like dried sponges, absorbing the liquidity the Fed provided to shore up their balance sheets and make up for rising losses, rather than releasing the cash into the economy. The Federal Reserve reported that in April, 55 percent of commercial banks were tightening lending standards on commercial loans, up from 30 percent in January. Finally, the market for the securitization and trading of debt—especially mortgage debt—ground to a halt. According to *Inside Mortgage Finance*, in the first three quarters of 2008, a mere $17 billion in subprime mortgages were made, down from $625 billion in 2006. The production of CDOs ceased altogether.

Problems began cropping up in the regulated banking sector. In July, IndyMac, the California-based bank that was a big player in Alt-A mortgages, was taken over by the Federal Deposit Insurance Corporation; it was the largest bank failure in twenty-four years and the second largest in history. FDIC chairwoman Sheila Bair, one of the few reality-based regulators, speaking at a confidence-building tour stop in Chicago, kept up a brave face. "The overwhelming majority of banks in this country continue to be well capitalized," she said. "My view is that I would be very, very surprised if an institution of significant size were to get into serious trouble." Just in case, though, the FDIC began hiring examiners and staffers experienced in bank closures out of retirement.

Pro Forma thinking was not banished totally, however. Economists polled by the Federal Reserve Bank of Philadelphia in May 2008 believed that the economy would grow at an annual rate of 1.7 percent and 1.8 percent in the third and fourth quarters, respectively. Nationwide, according to the S&P/Case-Shiller Home Price Index, home prices in the first quarter fell 14 percent from the year before. But Lawrence Yun, chief economist at the National Association of Realtors, said, "Home sales and prices in most of the country will improve during the second half of 2008."

Of course, home sales and prices did no such thing. And the economy *shrunk* in the second half of 2008. Further, the erosion of the housing market and the breakdown in the market for securitized debt spelled trouble for Fannie Mae and Freddie Mac, which, like the rest of the Shadow Banks, had thin layers of capital underlying lots of debt. In addition to issuing and insuring trillions of dollars in debt, Fannie and Freddie had purchased lots of mortgage-backed securities, including many backed by subprime loans. With $1.1 trillion of their securities resting on the balance sheets of foreign central banks, Fannie and Freddie were the ultimate Flat World/Network Finance businesses. As a result, their survival was a matter not just of economic policy, but also of foreign policy. So in July, as the two firms' capital positions eroded, Congress granted Henry Paulson the authority to come to the aid of Fannie Mae and Freddie Mac if needed. Not that it was needed just yet, Paulson noted. This was just a confidence-building move intended to ward off a Bear Stearns–like run on these Shadow Banks. "If you've got a bazooka, and people know you've got it, you may not have to take it out," Paulson said. But by the end of August, Paulson had to run to the arsenal to get heavier weaponry. With markets no longer willing to suspend their disbelief about the notion that the government would back the debt of Fannie and Freddie, on Sunday, September 7, the government essentially nationalized Fannie Mae and Freddie Mac, formally agreeing to backstop their debt and provide new capital. Why Sunday morning? The announcement was timed to hit the tape before the Asian markets opened for their Monday trading sessions.

In the next few weeks, the Shadow Banking system imploded. The failure of Fannie and Freddie led investors to freak out about the viability of highly indebted companies whose debt was not implicitly guaranteed by the government. Henry Paulson had told Lehman Brothers CEO Richard Fuld that the bank needed to find a buyer in the wake of new losses it had suffered. But European banks and private equity funds were licking their own self-inflicted wounds, and the Sovereign Wealth Funds had been burned. The investments they made in late 2007 and early 2008 were deep underwater. All the knife catchers had cut their hands badly. Lehman was unable to raise new capital and unable—or unwilling—to sharply reduce its high level of debt. And its senior executives seemed to spend more time blaming short-sellers for their woes and promising to get things under control than they did minding the store. "We have a long track record of pulling together when times are tough," Fuld said on a September 10 conference call with analysts. "We are on the right track to put these last two quarters behind us." Not so much. Lehman's numbers were staggering. It had $650 billion in debt outstanding and untold liabilities stemming from credit default swaps. During the crisis period of late August, a Lehman banker reportedly told government officials, "We have no idea of the details of our derivative exposure and neither do you." Yet Paulson, having come under fire for intervening on behalf of Bear Stearns, Fannie, and Freddie, decided to draw a line in the sand.

Denied help, Lehman Brothers filed for Chapter 11 on Monday, September 15. The failure signaled the end of investment banks acting like hedge funds. The remaining three mainstream Shadow Banks quickly changed stripes. Goldman Sachs and Morgan Stanley moved swiftly to transform into regulated commercial banks, which could accept deposits and borrow from the Federal Reserve and thus not have to rely on the capital markets exclusively for funding. They also raised new capital on tough terms from Warren Buffett (Goldman) and Mitsubishi UFJ (Morgan Stanley). Merrill Lynch CEO John Thain flipped off Fox News Channel long enough to find a Greater Fool: Bank of America CEO Kenneth Lewis. Lewis had already absorbed Countrywide, acquiring the whole company in June after the bank's initial investment tanked. Now Lewis, based in Charlotte, saw the opportunity to pick up a huge New York investment bank and the nation's largest stock brokerage force on the cheap. At a news conference at Bank of America's headquarters, which overlooked Bryant Park, Lewis crowed about Merrill's quality and headed off quickly to receive the ultimate middle-aged banker's prize: an exclusive interview with Maria Bartiromo of CNBC. While John Thain scurried off to deliver the bad news to Merrill, I could not help but think that Lewis was just another out-of-towner who had been pickpocketed near Times Square. As the nation's second-largest bank, Bank of America was beginning to confront its own problems with souring consumer credit. And here it was buying Merrill Lynch, which had billions of dollars of mortgage-backed securities, CDOs, and other exotica on its books? By January 2009, it was clear that Bank of America buying Merrill was like a boat taking on water believing it could save itself by lashing to another ship that was filling up with setting concrete.

The Bank of America–Merrill deal seemed like a footnote because all hell was breaking loose. The same week, AIG, whose Financial Products unit had pioneered the structured finance industry, was going under. AIG Financial Products had sold huge volumes of credit default swaps on subprime mortgages and was in deep trouble. Were it to fail, officials reasoned, AIG would pose the same systemic risk to the financial system that Bear Stearns and Lehman had. Using the Fannie-Freddie rescue as a template, Paulson hammered out an aggressive deal. He installed a new CEO and extended $85 billion in credit—at a high interest rate—in exchange for an 80 percent stake in the company. AIG's stock plummeted anyway.

The demise of Lehman Brothers, satisfying at first—it is about time somebody was allowed to fail!—quickly became deeply unsettling. How could they let Lehman Brothers fail? Analysts, officials, and investors seemed to be playing checkers on a three-dimensional chessboard. There was little appreciation for the knock-on effects of Lehman's failure. Much of Lehman's $650 billion in debt was held by money market funds, which were thought to be ultrasafe. And why wouldn't they hold Lehman paper? The 159-year-old firm was a pillar of the markets, and its debt was highly rated. But as fearful investors rushed to redeem shares in money market funds, that market froze up. So the Treasury Department temporarily extended insurance to money market funds, further expanding the government's footprint in the financial sector. Lehman was a big player in the commercial paper market, the vehicle through which companies borrow from investors on a short-term basis. Its bankruptcy helped stop the circulation of money through this vital blood-stream, requiring further government intervention.

The frenzy of failure culminated in late September with the passage of the $700 billion bailout bill. Yet the Troubled Asset Relief Program (TARP), which briefly disrupted the presidential campaign, was essentially stillborn. The original plan—to use taxpayer funds to buy toxic assets from the banks—was a non-starter precisely because of the degree to which Dumb Money had penetrated the financial sector. In theory, Treasury would buy the assets through some sort of auction. Given the lack of other buyers, and the desire to extract prices that would be re-motely fair to public taxpayers, Treasury would likely have had to set prices far below the values at which banks carried the as-sets on their books. Sales to Treasury thus would have estab-lished new, lower market prices for the assets, forcing banks and other financial firms to mark down their own holdings. And that only would have exacerbated existing problems with collateral and capital levels. So Paulson quickly abandoned the plan to buy assets and instead pursued a strategy of injecting capital directly into banks. The moves created a sense that Paulson and the Bush administration were simply lurching from crisis to crisis with-out a concrete plan. "We can spend a lot of time talking about how it happened and how we got here," Paulson told me. "But we have to get through the night first."

As the days shortened and the nights lengthened, that modest goal seemed increasingly difficult. The growing disconnect be-tween public rhetoric and actions and the apparent chaos in the streets undermined the most crucial factor in Network Finance: confidence. The whole sector was on fire, yet authorities asked people to remain calm. "We're very careful not to throw words around like 'meltdown' and 'free fall,'" CNN chief business cor-respondent Ali Velshi told the *New York Times*. The Rupert Murdoch–owned *Wall Street Journal* engaged in un-Murdochian restraint, banishing words like "crash" and "pandemonium."

The Securities and Exchange Commission awoke from its slumber to ban the short selling of financial stocks for thirty days. That did not work either.

To exacerbate matters, all the geniuses Dumb Money created began to look like idiots. In May, Carlyle Capital, the publicly held mortgage-backed hedge fund that used massive leverage, went out of business. With its stock at 30 cents, it was unwound—a black eye for its sponsor, the Carlyle Group. Hedge funds began to suffer. As wealthy people and institutions lost money, they began to yank money from hedge funds and from funds of funds. The result was a chain reaction of selling. To raise cash to pay investors, hedge funds sold shares, which begot lower prices, which caused more nervous investors to redeem. Rinse, lather, repeat. All of a sudden, this brilliant Dumb Money model—hedge funds were leveraged bets on leverage—seemed like a recipe for disaster. Remember 2 and 20? If your assets decline by half and there are no performance fees to be paid out, you are down to 1 and zero. A fund with $100 million under management that lost 50 percent of it assets would have only $500,000 to pay overhead and salaries for the year. By the end of 2008, hedge fund assets would fall to $1.4 trillion, according to Hedge Fund Research. The stock of the first major hedge fund to go public, Fortress Investment Group, fell from $30 in 2007 to 95 cents in December 2008, off 97 percent. Edward Lampert's mammoth buybacks of Sears proved to be foolhardy. Between the third quarter of 2005 and the third quarter of 2008, Sears spent $4.9 billion to buy 41.4 million of its own shares, at an average price of $118 per share. By the end of 2008, the stock stood at $41.

Private equity, another leveraged bet on leverage, began to lose its schwing as Erect Deal Dysfunction rose to epic levels. The volume of leveraged buyouts announced fell 84 percent, from $375 billion in 2007 to $61 billion in 2008. In addition, the market declines and freezing of credit meant that the avenues through which private equity realized profits—initial public of-

ferings, flipping companies to other buyers, dividend recapital-
izations—were all shut. In May 2008, Sam Zell managed to sell
Newsday to Cablevision for $650 million, but he had no luck
finding buyers quickly for the Chicago Cubs or the Tribune
Company's other trophy properties. The credit crunch decimated
the net worth of many potential buyers, and lenders fell by the
wayside. Having failed to find any Greater Fools, Tribune filed
for bankruptcy on December 8, 2008. Shares of the Blackstone
Group plummeted, falling below $5 per share in November 2008.
Many of the private equity–backed companies that issued payment-in-kind notes began to use the option to pay interest in
more debt rather than in cash. The owners of Freescale Semiconductor opted for payment in kind in December 2008. "Traditional private equity is dead and has been for a year," Leon Black,
founder of Apollo, told the *New York Times* in November 2008.
"It will probably remain so for a couple of years." Bill Conway,
chief investment officer, told Carlyle investors earlier the same
month: "You should expect very few distributions from us."
Yale's alternative asset heavy endorsement lost nearly 25 percent of its value in the second half of 2008.

Yet the old ways of thinking died hard. The addiction to
Cheap Money proved difficult to kick. The home-building lobby
begged Congress to give tax breaks to people to buy new homes,
which would have been a little like treating a hangover by doing
a few shots, shotgunning a can of beer, then busting out the funnel that can handle two beers at a time. Wall Street firms, which
had literally become wards of the state, were unable to understand why they should reduce bonuses. Walking around mid-
town Manhattan I began to feel like Haley Joel Osment's boy
psychic in *The Sixth Sense*. "I see dead investment banks." John
Thain thought he deserved a $10 million bonus for selling Mer-
rill to Bank of America, even though, as a result of the acquisi-
tion, Bank of America would soon have to seek more government
support.

In the fall, the crisis entered the Alanis Morissette phase. You would pick up the *Wall Street Journal* every morning and ask, Isn't that ironic? WCI, the home builder that had dismissed Carl Icahn's $22 a share in April 2007 as inadequate, filed for bankruptcy in August 2008. In November, Texas-based Franklin Bank—founded by Lew Ranieri, who had helped invent the mortgage-backed security in the 1980s—failed and cost the FDIC insurance fund $1.4 billion to $1.6 billion. Alan Greenspan detected a flaw in his ideology. Some billionaires, it was revealed, were no better at managing their financial affairs than unqualified home buyers. They lived as if they had $1 billion in the bank instead of $1 billion in stock, borrowing heavily to support their lifestyles. Sumner Redstone, the founder of Viacom, who had borrowed against his holdings, was forced to sell millions of shares in CBS and Viacom when he received a margin call. Pete Peterson, a founder of the Blackstone Group, deployed some of his debt-based fortune to back a documentary about the perils of debt: *I.O.U.S.A.* The Shadow Banking system went from a mutual aid society to circular firing squad. J.P. Morgan, it was alleged, had helped hasten Lehman's demise by demanding Lehman post collateral. Hedge funds aggressively sold short the stocks of Goldman Sachs and Morgan Stanley. Citigroup, a barely solvent bank, put the screws to General Growth Properties, a barely solvent mall developer. Ben Bernanke's ballpark continued to expand. Bloomberg News reported that between January 2007 and November 2008, credit losses for banks had topped $918 billion. In October, the International Monetary Fund raised its estimate of total loss from $945 billion in April 2008 to $1.4 trillion. Losses were now "contained" to Spain, which had its own housing bubble and credit collapse, to Switzerland, whose ultracautious banking system suffered grievous losses, and to the entire nation of Iceland, which went bankrupt.

As the year spun to a close, the damage began to appear in the real economy. Take away leverage, and a power lifter becomes a ninety-eight-pound weakling. Suddenly, consumers realized that if they wanted something—a car, clothes, a vacation—they would have to pay for it. Credit card companies, which were also members of the Shadow Banking system and relied on Network Finance, began reducing lines of credit. With housing prices falling, there was less home equity to borrow against or monetize. In the first three quarters of 2008, Americans took out $102 billion in HELOCs, compared with $430 billion for all of 2006. Refinancings were running at less than half the 2005 pace. Retailers reported greater use of debit cards and less use of credit cards. Christmas sales fell across the board. The economy's biggest and traditionally most leveraged purchases—the original Cheap Money businesses—fell of a cliff. Car sales fell 18 percent in 2008, and existing-home sales fell 13.1 percent from the year before.

The implosion of Dumb Money businesses erased much of the economic progress of the decade. By the end of 2008, stocks had fallen back to where they were in 1997. The foreclosure epidemic took the home ownership rate in the third quarter of 2008 back to its 2002 level. Household net worth plummeted from its peak of $62.6 trillion in the third quarter of 2007 to $56.5 trillion in the third quarter of 2008, below the level of 2005.

As a new year dawned, and a new administration stood ready to inherit a financial and economic mess unseen since 1933, it was clear that the Era of Dumb Money was over.

Conclusion

Here is where the author, having smugly diagnosed a nation's woes with perfect hindsight, offers a ten-point, 1,500-word plan that will fix everything. There should be some reward for the stalwarts who soldiered through the first eight chapters. I hate to disappoint, but the situation is so fluid that any program proposed in January is likely to be rendered unworkable in March. I do, however, have some concluding thoughts.

Throughout this book, I have deemphasized, perhaps downplayed, the role and influence of regulation in the Era of Dumb Money. It is tempting to blame the immolations of Fannie Mae and Freddie Mac, and the systemic problems, on poor government oversight. And there is no doubt this was part of the problem. Even discounting the fact that he was a Bush appointee, Christopher Cox was an ineffectual SEC head. When it came to the dangers posed by the new financial order, Federal Reserve chairman Greenspan was Mr. Magoo. The Bush administration and the Federal Reserve, as a matter of ideology, thought less regulation was better. The refusal to crack down on subprime lending or to regulate Shadow Banks was of a piece with the prevailing philosophy in the executive branch and in the independent Fed. But a colder calculation than mere ideology was at work. Simply put, both political parties were favorably disposed to the Dumb Money industries. The Clinton administration and the leading congressional Democrats in the age of Bush were friendly to Wall Street for personal and political reasons. Many of the leading lights of the party, especially those who dealt with financial regulation—senators Chris Dodd of Connecticut and

Chuck Schumer of New York—hailed from Greater Hedgistan. The campaigns of both Hillary Clinton and Barack Obama were backed profusely by Hedge Fund Nation.

Would better or more aggressive regulations have made a difference? Sure, it would have. But to a degree, that is a counterfactual argument. In our system, the financial services industry tends to get exactly the amount of regulation it wants. Wall Street got everything it wanted from Washington in the past ten years, going back to the second Clinton administration: cuts in capital gains tax, ending Glass-Steagall (the legislation enacted in 1933 to separate investment and commercial banks), and more cuts on capital gains and dividends. That is one of many reasons the right-wing drive to blame the whole mess on the Community Reinvestment Act, which was intended to address discrimination in lending, is so bogus. Banks were not slavish followers of a Washington regulatory regime. Rather, Washington was a slavish follower of the banks' regulatory regime.

When it cannot influence the final formulation of policy, Wall Street frequently manages to execute an end run around whatever new rules are set up. Define a practice as regulated or proscribed, and a lawyer will craft a new practice that allows companies to do essentially the same thing. After Congress struck a blow against excessive executive pay in the early 1990s by limiting the deductibility of salaries greater than $1 million, companies dispensed stock options by the gazillions. After regulators struck a blow against excessive executive pay in the early years of this decade, by requiring the expensing of options, companies dispensed restricted stock by the gazillions. Limit bonuses and golden parachutes for CEOs, and Wall Street firms will simply boost the guaranteed component of compensation.

Regulators always try to regulate against the last debacle. After a slew of accounting scandals, Congress in 2002 passed the Sarbanes-Oxley Act, which correctly forced CEOs to sign off on the accuracy of financial statements. That did not help ward off this financial crisis. The problems in the past year have very little to do with fudged numbers. Everything was done pretty much in the open, and the quarterly numbers were largely accurate. Investors had simply convinced themselves that we should ignore the vast levels of debt that Shadow Banks held and instead focus on Value at Risk. Pro Forma thinking told them that the capital structures were manageable because asset prices would not fall. Sure, the mortgage industry produced a fair number of crooks. But they were mostly responsible for small-time bad acts. In the case of the biggest and most expensive systemic failures—Lehman Brothers, AIG, Fannie and Freddie—managers were craven, stupid, and incompetent, but not probably criminals.

Markets already have started doing much of the heavy lifting of retroactive regulations. There have been calls to regulate the credit default swaps market and make it more transparent. That is starting to happen with the emergence of a central clearing exchange. There have been calls to rein in private equity and hedge funds from buying companies. The closing of the high-yield bond market has taken care of that. Leverage limits for big unregulated investment banks? Done. (There are no more big unregulated investment banks.) Rules that prohibit houses being bought with no money down and no-documentation mortgages? All those lenders are gone.

What's more, it is impossible at some level to regulate speculation. The only way to prevent a recurrence of something like the Dumb Money debacle is to outlaw or regulate stupidity. It is very difficult for any institution or person to prevent a bubble. Alan Greenspan says that he tried a bit in the 1990s. "We tightened the economy quite significantly at various times during the 1990s, and rather than defuse the bubble, we enhanced it," he told me in October 2007. But when interest rates are your main tool, he continued, "You can only break a bubble if you break the underlying basis of the economy."

So if we cannot rely on regulations or monetary policy, can we rely on human intelligence? At first blush, the answer would seem to be no. Bubbles speak to something innate in the American psyche. They are fun. They make a lot of people feel rich. They generate enthusiasm. And they are contagious. If one business idea works, five hundred other people will try it. Somebody is always willing to start, and to finance, the eighth online pet store, the 7,567th hedge fund, the 137th condo tower in Miami, and the 52nd ethanol plant. The same dynamics—Pro Forma thinking, the concoction of new theories to fit seemingly irrational facts—happened before the Era of Dumb Money, and they will happen again soon. Once an economic trend gets going, it is difficult to stop. Look no further than the alternative energy sector or the government bond market.

In addition, once a trend stops, it reverses quickly. A bubble breaks, Greenspan said, when it becomes clear that long-term expectations are patently unrealistic. "The result of this is a dramatic 180-degree switch that goes from exuberance to fear." We go from an environment where anybody will lend any amount of money to anybody (2006) to one in which nobody will lend to any amount of money to anybody (2009). Far from being continually rational, the economy and our markets are frequently bipolar. We need a sort of fiscal lithium, an agent that smoothes out things. It might take away some of our personality and make us a little less fun to be around, but it will also make us less destructive and easier to live with.

Another way of putting it is that we need to be less procyclical. Since apparently we cannot stop ourselves from pressing the pedal to the metal when we are excited, perhaps we need some automatic brakes. When a bubble gets going, all the incentives—financial, social, cultural, political—push in the same direction. Those who embrace the mentality of the bubble with the most fervor are richly rewarded, while the more cautious are punished. During the Era of Dumb Money, the more you borrowed to make bets on companies and stocks, the more money you made and the more social and cultural capital you accumulated. The more political capital, too. When it attains critical mass, the first thing an industry does is form a lobby to ask for more help and subsidies and to ward off regulation. This dynamic helps explain why too much of our policy is procyclical. Every year that housing prices rose, Fannie Mae and Freddie Mac raised their loan limits, making it possible for people to borrow more and push prices higher. The home mortgage deduction is similarly procyclical. The more you borrow, the more taxpayers subsidized your speculation. The fact that gains from hedge funds and private equity transactions were taxed at a significantly lower rate than ordinary income helped propel growth into those sectors. The FDIC stopped collecting insurance premiums when times were good, so long as the funds on hand amounted to 1.25 percent of insured deposits—no matter how much banks expanded. (It is as if companies stopped selling flood insurance after three years had passed without a hurricane.)

As we consider reforms to all these sectors, we have to think about ways to make regulation more countercyclical. The best time to tell banks to boost their reserves is during a boom, when their balance sheets are expanding and they have easy access to capital—not after they have collapsed. The banks resisted deposit insurance in the 1930s. And the Shadow Banks, private equity funds, insurance firms, hedge funds, and large pools of capital would have fought any mandate to insure themselves from failure. Given the fact that many are now dependent on the government, they have lost their right to a significant voice in public policy. Clearly, derivatives and securitization alone are not sufficient insurance. But what if the asset management industry effectively insured itself against meltdowns? A tax on securities trading and the creation and trading of structured financial products could go into a stabilization fund that would serve as bubble insurance, which is essentially what deposit insurance is. Funds thus raised could also be used to defray some of the enormous costs of the bailout. As the free-market economists say: If you want less of something, tax it.

Most important, we simply have to be smarter—as individuals, investors, managers, and citizens. The reality is that we are neither as smart as we think we are during the peaks nor as stupid as we think we are during the troughs. Nonetheless, we have to be a little more willing to be stupid during Dumb Money eras, to leave money on the table, to forego the easy returns our friends and neighbors are making, to be a little less trendy, to be the one firm that does not plunge into subprime. We must be more self-aware. By now, we should be able to recognize the features and stages of bubbles—the initial enthusiasm, the spread of Pro Forma thinking, the shark-jumping moments—and try harder not to get caught up. Here is a handy rule of thumb. If you catch yourself parroting lines spoken by analysts on CNBC—i.e., if you caught yourself discussing the per-eyeball valuation of Amazon.com in 1999 or found yourself in 2006 rationalizing the purchase of a third house with the intention of flipping it—that's a pretty good sign you are in a bubble.

The End of Dumb Money has been like a death—of dozens of institutions, thousands of careers, millions of dreams, and billions in value. Just so, as we grapple with the aftermath, we seem to be proceeding through the five stages of grief. First came denial, which was rampant throughout the system. Next came anger at the size and manner of the bailouts. Third, bargaining: last fall, it was common to hear arguments that taxpayers might actually make money on the bailout. And around December, the fourth stage, depression, set in. It still lingers. I hope that is where it stops. For it would be a shame if we moved on quickly to the final stage, acceptance. There is nothing acceptable about what happened. Despite what the Smart Money crowd argued—despite Donald Trump's assertion of a *force majeure*, Robert Rubin's insistence of inevitability, and Alan Greenspan's concession of a minor flaw in ideology—this crisis was not a random, once-in-a-lifetime thing that fell out of the sky. It was a man-made product that turned out to be immensely toxic and damaging. And we'll be paying for the cleanup for a long time.

Acknowledgments

This book came together in a matter of weeks but was several years in the making. I am grateful to the many people who made it possible.

Bits and pieces of this volume—anecdotes, ideas, themes, the odd paragraph—appeared in many different venues over the years. I am grateful to the editors at several publications who improved and helped refine my ideas. Thanks, then, to Hugo Lindgren at *New York* and Jeff Sommer at *The New York Times*. Since I began writing for *Slate* in the summer of 2002, David Plotz has edited hundreds of my columns with a sharp eye and good cheer. I have also benefited from the counsel and input of *Slate* colleagues June Thomas, Jacob Weisberg, and James Ledbetter from the work of *Slate*'s copy desk. Joining *Newsweek* in the summer of 2007 not only gave me a front-row seat to the emerging crisis, it also forced me to do some reporting and enabled me to meet many of the key players. I am grateful for the gentle supervision, fine editing, and constant support and encouragement of David Jefferson, Kathy Deveny, David Kaplan, Arlyn Gajilan, and Jon Meacham. *Newsweek* reporters Daniel Stone, Matthew Philips, Temma Ehrenfeld, Ashley Harris, and Barrett Sheridan made significant contributions to many of the articles on which this book is based. Karim Bardeesy corrected many errors and hunted down stray facts.

My agent, Sloan Harris, at ICM, was the first to latch on to the possibilities of an electronic book. Once again, he helped mold some inchoate thoughts into a finished product with enthusiasm and skill.

The entire team at the Free Press, led by Dominick Anfuso, and Martha Levin, threw the rulebook out the window to produce this book practically overnight. Sharbari Bose and Leah Miller shepherded the book through the stages of publication, Eric Fuentecilla designed the clever cover, and Patricia Romanowski copyedited the book with skill and care.

The burdens of book writing always fall heaviest on family members, who have to endure the presence (and frequent absence) of a distracted mope in the house. My thanks to my children, Aliza and Ethan, for their patience, their spirit, and their curiosity.

Most of all, my thanks again to my partner and best friend, Candice Savin. Her good humor, diligence, love, and optimism make my life full and are a continual source of inspiration.